WIDER THAN THE SKY

Poems to Grow Up With

WIDER THAN THE SKY

Poems to Grow Up With

COLLECTED AND EDITED BY

SCOTT ELLEDGE

Harper & Row, Publishers

WIDER THAN THE SKY: *Poems To Grow Up With*
Copyright © 1990 by Scott Elledge

Library of Congress Cataloging-in-Publication Data
Wider than the sky : poems to grow up with / collected and edited by
    Scott Elledge.
        p.   cm.
    Includes bibliographical references.
    Summary: A diverse anthology of poems by William Shakespeare, Dr.
Seuss, Emily Dickinson, and many others.
    ISBN 0-06-021786-3. — ISBN 0-06-021787-1 (lib. bdg.)
    1. Children's poetry, English.   2. Children's poetry, American.
[1. English poetry—Collections.   2. American poetry—Collections.]
I. Elledge, Scott.
PR1175.3.W55   1990   90-4135
821.008′09282—dc20   CIP
                                                            AC

10 9 8 7 6 5 4 3 2 1
First Edition

"Poetry and hums aren't things which you get, they're things which get *you*. And all you can do is to go where they can find you."

—WINNIE-THE-POOH

TABLE OF CONTENTS

PREFACE

I originally collected these poems for an anthology I made one summer for a ten-year-old niece. When I came upon a poem I liked and thought she would like, I photocopied it on a sheet of good bond paper, and at the end of the summer I bound the sheets in bright-blue buckram, had her name printed in gold on the cover, and sent it to her in time for her birthday. Of course I hoped my present would please her right off, but I also hoped it would, during the next few years, help her discover the wide world that is open to all who love poetry.

In my "Preface," I said I hoped she would enjoy reading poems in a book that had no illustrations to distract her attention from the spellbinding, or enchanting, effects produced by beautiful works of art made solely with words. At her age she no longer wanted artists, no matter how gifted, interpreting her poems for her, or visualizing their content, before she'd had a chance to do so for herself. And I added that I hoped she would enjoy the random order in which the poems appeared, following one another haphazardly, like the faces of people coming up out of the subway or down the escalator at the airport.

I hoped she wouldn't mind my giving her three hints about how to read poems. One, don't force yourself to read poems that fail to catch your fancy right off. You can try them again next month, or next year. Two, don't stop reading a poem you like when you hit a word or passage you can't quite understand—hang in, hang on, the way you do when listening to (or overhearing) someone who seems to be (but probably isn't) speaking over your head. Keep trying to get the drift, the way you have been doing ever since the day you began to learn our language. If, having finished the poem, you still rather like it, but are still puzzled, you may wish to look in the back of the book, where, like a professor, I have added a few Explanatory Notes. Three, and most of all, I said, take time to listen to the poems, to hear yourself reading them, because much of a poem's meaning, as well as its charm, comes from its sound.

Until about five hundred years ago poetry was seldom read silently and privately; it was usually chanted, sung, or read aloud in public. A poetry reading was more like a recital or a performance than a meditation. For about two thousand years the speeches in plays were written in metrical language, and the plays were performed, of course, by professional actors, whose art lay mainly in their ability to "speak the speech trippingly on the tongue," as Hamlet put it. Narrative poems (epics and ballads) were chanted or sung to an audience by "singers," who were required to have a good ear and a good voice, as well as a good memory. Ballads and folk songs were also sung by amateurs, by anyone who could carry the tune and remember the words—and probably by some who couldn't, or at least not very well.

Before the invention of printing, shorter poems, or "lyrics," such as most of the poems in this book, were published by word of mouth, or written out by hand and passed around among friends. The first printed book of poems in English, a "miscellany" of poems by various leading poets of the time, appeared in 1557; and since then reading poetry has gradually become a private rather than a social pleasure, and a poem's "audience" now consists usually of one reader at a time.

Good readers read poetry the way musicians read music—for the fun of listening to it during the process of understanding it. Though most of the poems in this collection are not hard to understand, you will find poems whose meanings are not simple or clear, and in reading these poems you may occasionally discover that you are being attracted to a poem before you have quite understood it.

That won't seem strange if you have ever fallen in love with a person (or a thing) when you had only the faintest idea of what he or she (or it) was really like. After all, there is no law that says you have to understand people before you can fall in love with them. And when you think about it, "love at first sight" doesn't necessarily mean you were attracted by what you *saw.* In poetry, as often as not, it's what you *hear,* not what you *see* (or understand) that makes your heart thump, or makes you feel a little giddy and out of breath.

Dangerous as it sometimes proves to be, hardly anything beats falling in love, and falling in love at first sight is not uncommon. Every split second someone, somewhere, falls in love at first sight. The phenomenon is not as common as, let's say, finding dandelions, but it is not as uncommon as finding an orchid in your backyard or running into a saint. With a little luck, you'll find an irresistible poem the first or second time you explore this collection. Just remember that finding and falling for an enchanting poem is, like falling in love at first sight, something you can't make happen. All you can do is follow the advice of that famous poet Winnie-the-Pooh, who, when Eeyore asked him how he "got" all the fine poems that seemed to pop out of him spontaneously, answered: "Poetry and hums aren't things which you get; they're things which get *you.*"

Though some of the poems in this book were written for children, most of them were written for adults. But that's no reason why young readers should not read them. Thinking you have to be an adult to understand poems written for adults is like thinking you have to be an adult to understand adults, or a boy to understand boys, or an Indian to understand Indians. One way to understand adults, or members of another sex or nation, is to read the poems they write.

I hope that those who have read this preface will now begin to browse in the collection itself, and that some of them will find, like the poetical tortoise in the lettuce bed (see page 124), that

> One cannot have enough
> Of this delicious stuff!

Scott Elledge
Ithaca, New York
June 1, 1990

WIDER THAN THE SKY

Poems to Grow Up With

Poetry

What is Poetry? Who knows?
Not a rose, but the scent of the rose;
Not the sky, but the light in the sky;
Not the fly, but the gleam of the fly;
Not the sea, but the sound of the sea;
Not myself, but what makes me
See, hear, and feel something that prose
Cannot: and what it is, who knows?

ELEANOR FARJEON

Sea Shell

Sea Shell, Sea Shell,
    Sing me a song, O please!
A song of ships, and sailor men,
    And parrots, and tropical trees,

Of islands lost in the Spanish Main
Which no man ever may find again,
Of fishes and corals under the waves,
And sea horses stabled in great green caves.

Sea Shell, Sea Shell,
Sing of the things you know so well.

AMY LOWELL

The Chipmunk's Day

In and out the bushes, up the ivy,
Into the hole
By the old oak stump, the chipmunk flashes.
Up the pole

To the feeder full of seeds he dashes,
Stuffs his cheeks,
The chickadee and titmouse scold him.
Down he streaks.

Red as the leaves the wind blows off the maple,
Red as a fox,
Striped like a skunk, the chipmunk whistles
Past the love seat, past the mailbox,

Down the path,
Home to his warm hole stuffed with sweet
Things to eat.
Neat and slight and shining, his front feet

Curled at his breast, he sits there while the sun
Stripes the red west
With its last light: the chipmunk
Dives to his rest.

RANDALL JARRELL

Kidnap Poem

ever been kidnapped
by a poet
if i were a poet
i'd kidnap you
put you in my phrases and meter
you to jones beach
or maybe coney island
or maybe just to my house
lyric you in lilacs
dash you in the rain
blend into the beach
to complement my see
play the lyre for you
ode you with my love song
anything to win you
wrap you in the red Black green
show you off to mama
yeah if i were a poet i'd kid
nap you

NIKKI GIOVANNI

The Brain—is wider than the Sky—
For—put them side by side—
The one the other will contain
With ease—and You—beside—

The Brain is deeper than the sea—
For—hold them—Blue to Blue—
The one the other will absorb—
As Sponges—Buckets—do—

The Brain is just the weight of God—
For—Heft them—Pound for Pound—
And they will differ—if they do—
As Syllable from Sound—

EMILY DICKINSON

Down by the Salley Gardens

Down by the salley gardens my love and I did meet;
She passed the salley gardens with little snow-white feet.
She bid me take love easy, as the leaves grow on the tree;
But I, being young and foolish, with her would not agree.

In a field by the river my love and I did stand,
And on my leaning shoulder she laid her snow-white hand.
She bid me take life easy, as the grass grows on the weirs;
But I was young and foolish, and now am full of tears.

WILLIAM BUTLER YEATS

Cockles and Mussels

In Dublin's fair city, where the girls are so pretty,
I first set my eyes on sweet Mollie Malone,
As she wheeled her wheel-barrow through streets broad and
    narrow,
Crying, "Cockles and mussels: alive, alive O!"

She was a fishmonger, but sure 'twas no wonder,
For so were her father and mother before;
They wheeled a wheel-barrow through streets broad and narrow,
Crying, "Cockles and mussels: alive, alive O!"

She died of a fever, and no one could save her,
And that was the end of sweet Mollie Malone;
Now a ghost wheels her barrow through streets broad and
    narrow,
Crying, "Cockles and mussels: alive, alive O!"

ANONYMOUS

Spruce Woods

It's so still
today that a
dipping bough means
a squirrel
has gone through.

A. R. AMMONS

All day I hear the noise of waters
    Making moan,
Sad as the sea-bird is, when going
    Forth alone,
He hears the winds cry to the waters'
    Monotone.

The gray winds, the cold winds are blowing
    Where I go.
I hear the noise of many waters
    Far below.
All day, all night, I hear them flowing
    To and fro.

JAMES JOYCE

First Sight

Lambs that learn to walk in snow
When their bleating clouds the air
Meet a vast unwelcome, know
Nothing but a sunless glare.
Newly stumbling to and fro
All they find, outside the fold,
Is a wretched width of cold.

As they wait beside the ewe,
Her fleeces wetly caked, there lies
Hidden round them, waiting too,
Earth's immeasurable surprise.
They could not grasp it if they knew,
What so soon will wake and grow
Utterly unlike the snow.

PHILIP LARKIN

The Frog

Be kind and tender to the Frog,
  And do not call him names,
As "Slimy-skin," or "Polly-wog,"
  Or likewise "Ugly James,"
Or "Gap-a-grin," or "Toad-gone-wrong,"
  Or "Bill Bandy-knees":
The Frog is justly sensitive
  To epithets like these.
No animal will more repay
  A treatment kind and fair;
At least so lonely people say
Who keep a frog (and, by the way,
They are extremely rare).

HILAIRE BELLOC

Incident

(FOR ERIC WALROND)

Once riding in old Baltimore,
    Heart-filled, head-filled with glee,
I saw a Baltimorean
    Keep looking straight at me.

Now I was eight and very small,
    And he was no whit bigger,
And so I smiled, but he poked out
    His tongue, and called me, "Nigger."

I saw the whole of Baltimore
    From May until December;
Of all the things that happened there
    That's all that I remember.

                              COUNTEE CULLEN

The Country Mouse and the City Mouse

In a snug little cot lived a fat little mouse,
Who enjoyed, unmolested, the range of the house;
With plain food content, she would breakfast on cheese,
She dined upon bacon, and supped on gray peas.

A friend from the town to the cottage did stray,
And he said he was come a short visit to pay;
So the mouse spread her table as gay as you please,
And brought the nice bacon and charming gray peas.

The visitor frowned, and he thought to be witty:
Cried he, "You must know, I am come from the city,
Where we all should be shocked at provisions like these,
For we never eat bacon and horrid gray peas.

"To town come with me, I will give you a treat:
Some excellent food, most delightful to eat.
With me shall you feast just as long as you please;
Come, leave this fat bacon and shocking gray peas."

This kind invitation she could not refuse,
And the city mouse wished not a moment to lose;
Reluctant she quitted the fields and the trees,
The delicious fat bacon and charming gray peas.

They slily crept under a gay parlor door,
Where a feast had been given the evening before;
And it must be confessed they on dainties did seize,
Far better than bacon, or even gray peas.

Here were custard and trifle, and cheesecakes good store,
Nice sweetmeats and jellies, and twenty things more;
All that art had invented the palate to please,
Except some fat bacon and smoking gray peas.

They were nicely regaling, when into the room
Came the dog and the cat, and the maid with a broom:
They jumped in a custard both up to their knees;
The country mouse sighed for her bacon and peas.

Cried she to her friend, "Get me safely away,
I can venture no longer in London to stay;
For if oft you receive interruptions like these,
Give me my nice bacon and charming gray peas.

"Your living is splendid and gay, to be sure,
But the dread of disturbance you ever endure;
I taste true delight in contentment and ease,
And I *feast* on fat bacon and charming gray peas."

RICHARD SCRAFTON SHARPE

The Giraffes

I think before they saw me the giraffes
Were watching me. Over the golden grass,
The bush and ragged open tree of thorn,
From a grotesque height, under their lightish horns,
Their eyes were fixed on mine as I approached them.
The hills behind descended steeply: iron-
Colored outcroppings of rock half-covered by
Dull green and sepia vegetation, dry
And sunlit: and above, the piercing blue
Where clouds like islands lay or like swans flew.

Seen from those hills the scrubby plain is like
A large-scale map whose features have a look
Half menacing, half familiar, and across
Its brightness arms of shadow ceaselessly
Revolve. Like small forked twigs or insects move
Giraffes, upon the great map where they live.

When I went nearer, their long bovine tails
Flicked loosely, and deliberately they turned,
An undulation of dappled gray and brown,
And stood in profile with those curious planes
Of neck and sloping haunches. Just as when,
Quite motionless, they watched I never thought
Them moved by fear, a wish to be a tree,
So as they put more ground between us I
Saw evidence that these were animals
With no desire for intercourse, or no
Capacity.
              Above the falling sun,
Like visible winds the clouds are streaked and spun,
And cold and dark now bring the image of
Those creatures walking without pain or love.

ROY FULLER

Stopping by Woods on a Snowy Evening

Whose woods these are I think I know.
His house is in the village, though;
He will not see me stopping here
To watch his woods fill up with snow.

My little horse must think it queer
To stop without a farmhouse near
Between the woods and frozen lake
The darkest evening of the year.

He gives his harness bells a shake
To ask if there is some mistake.
The only other sound's the sweep
Of easy wind and downy flake.

The woods are lovely, dark and deep,
But I have promises to keep,
And miles to go before I sleep,
And miles to go before I sleep.

ROBERT FROST

When We Two Parted

When we two parted
    In silence and tears,
Half broken-hearted
    To sever for years,
Pale grew thy cheek and cold,
    Colder thy kiss;
Truly that hour foretold
    Sorrow to this.

The dew of the morning
    Sunk chill on my brow—
It felt like the warning
    Of what I feel now.
Thy vows are all broken,
    And light is thy fame;
I hear thy name spoken,
    And share in its shame.

They name thee before me,
    A knell to mine ear;
A shudder comes o'er me—
    Why wert thou so dear?
They know not I knew thee,
    Who knew thee too well—
Long, long shall I rue thee,
    Too deeply to tell.

In secret we met—
    In silence I grieve,
That thy heart could forget,
    Thy spirit deceive.
If I should meet thee
    After long years,
How should I greet thee?—
    With silence and tears.

GEORGE GORDON, LORD BYRON

I Wandered Lonely as a Cloud

I wandered lonely as a cloud
That floats on high o'er vales and hills,
When all at once I saw a crowd,
A host, of golden daffodils;
Beside the lake, beneath the trees,
Fluttering and dancing in the breeze.

Continuous as the stars that shine
And twinkle on the milky way,
They stretched in never-ending line
Along the margin of a bay:
Ten thousand saw I at a glance,
Tossing their heads in sprightly dance.

The waves beside them danced; but they
Outdid the sparkling waves in glee;
A poet could not but be gay,
In such a jocund company;
I gazed—and gazed—but little thought
What wealth the show to me had brought:

For oft, when on my couch I lie
In vacant or in pensive mood,
They flash upon that inward eye
Which is the bliss of solitude;
And then my heart with pleasure fills,
And dances with the daffodils.

WILLIAM WORDSWORTH

What Are Heavy?

What are heavy? Sea-sand and sorrow;
What are brief? Today and tomorrow;
What are frail? Spring blossoms and youth;
What are deep? The ocean and truth.

CHRISTINA ROSSETTI

Good Morrow

Pack, clouds, away! and welcome, day!
   With night we banish sorrow.
Sweet air, blow soft; mount, lark, aloft
   To give my love good morrow.
Wings from the wind to please her mind,
   Notes from the lark I'll borrow:
Bird, prune thy wing, nightingale, sing,
   To give my love good morrow!
     To give my love good morrow
     Notes from them all I'll borrow.

Wake from thy nest, robin redbreast!
   Sing, birds, in every furrow
And from each bill let music shrill
   Give my fair love good morrow.
Blackbird and thrush in every bush,
   Stare, linnet, and cock-sparrow,
You pretty elves, amongst yourselves
   Sing my fair love good morrow.
     To give my love good morrow
     Sing, birds, in every furrow.

THOMAS HEYWOOD

How do I love thee? Let me count the ways.
  I love thee to the depth and breadth and height
  My soul can reach, when feeling out of sight
For the ends of Being and ideal Grace.
I love thee to the level of every day's
  Most quiet need, by sun and candlelight.
  I love thee freely, as men strive for Right;
I love thee purely, as they turn from Praise.
I love thee with the passion put to use
  In my old griefs, and with my childhood's faith.
I love thee with a love I seemed to lose
  With my lost saints,—I love thee with the breath,
Smiles, tears, of all my life!—and, if God choose,
  I shall but love thee better after death.

ELIZABETH BARRETT BROWNING

The Passionate Shepherd to His Love

Come live with me and be my love,
And we will all the pleasures prove
That valleys, groves, hills, and fields,
Woods, or steepy mountain yields.

And we will sit upon the rocks,
Seeing the shepherds feed their flocks,
By shallow rivers to whose falls
Melodious birds sing madrigals.

And I will make thee beds of roses
And a thousand fragrant posies,
A cap of flowers, and a kirtle
Embroidered all with leaves of myrtle;

A gown made of the finest wool
Which from our pretty lambs we pull;
Fair lined slippers for the cold,
With buckles of the purest gold;

A belt of straw and ivy buds,
With coral clasps and amber studs:
And if these pleasures may thee move,
Come live with me, and be my love.

The shepherds' swains shall dance and sing
For thy delight each May morning:
If these delights thy mind may move,
Then live with me and be my love.

CHRISTOPHER MARLOWE

The Nymph's Reply to the Shepherd

If all the world and love were young,
And truth in every shepherd's tongue,
These pretty pleasures might me move
To live with thee and be thy love.

Time drives the flocks from field to fold
When rivers rage and rocks grow cold,
And Philomel becometh dumb;
The rest complains of cares to come.

The flowers do fade, and wanton fields
To wayward winter reckoning yields;
A honey tongue, a heart of gall,
Is fancy's spring, but sorrow's fall.

Thy gowns, thy shoes, thy beds of roses,
Thy cap, thy kirtle, and thy posies
Soon break, soon wither, soon forgotten—
In folly ripe, in reason rotten.

Thy belt of straw and ivy buds,
Thy coral clasps and amber studs,
All these in me no means can move
To come to thee and be thy love.

But could youth last and love still breed,
Had joys no date nor age no need,
Then these delights my mind might move
To live with thee and be thy love.

SIR WALTER RALEGH

August

The sprinkler twirls.
    The summer wanes.
The pavement wears
    Popsicle stains.

The playground grass
    Is worn to dust.
The weary swings
    Creak, creak with rust.

The trees are bored
    With being green.
Some people leave
    The local scene

And go to seaside
    Bungalows
And take off nearly
    All their clothes.

JOHN UPDIKE

Those Winter Sundays

Sundays too my father got up early
and put his clothes on in the blueblack cold,
then with cracked hands that ached
from labor in the weekday weather made
banked fires blaze. No one ever thanked him.

I'd wake and hear the cold splintering, breaking.
When the rooms were warm, he'd call,
and slowly I would rise and dress,
fearing the chronic angers of that house,

Speaking indifferently to him,
who had driven out the cold
and polished my good shoes as well.
What did I know, what did I know
of love's austere and lonely offices?

ROBERT HAYDEN

The Rabbit

When they said the time to hide was mine,
I hid back under a thick grape vine.

And while I was still for the time to pass,
A little gray thing came out of the grass.

He hopped his way through the melon bed
And sat down close by a cabbage head.

He sat down close where I could see,
And his big still eyes looked hard at me,

His big eyes bursting out of the rim,
And I looked back very hard at him.

ELIZABETH MADOX ROBERTS

Reason

Said, Pull her up a bit will you, Mac, I want to unload there.
Said, Pull her up my rear end, first come first serve.
Said, Give her the gun, Bud, he needs a taste of his own
     bumper.
Then the usher came out and got into the act:

Said, Pull her up, pull her up a bit, we need this space, sir.
Said, For God's sake, is this still a free country or what?
You go back and take care of Gary Cooper's horse
And leave me handle my own car.

Saw them unloading the lame old lady,
Ducked out under the wheel and gave her an elbow,
Said, All you needed to do was just explain;
Reason, Reason is my middle name.

JOSEPHINE MILES

May

I cannot tell you how it was;
But this I know: it came to pass—
Upon a bright and breezy day
When May was young; ah, pleasant May!
As yet the poppies were not born
Between the blades of tender corn;
The last eggs had not hatched as yet,
Nor any bird foregone its mate.

I cannot tell you what it was;
But this I know: it did but pass.
It passed away with sunny May,
With all sweet things it passed away,
And left me old, and cold, and gray.

CHRISTINA ROSSETTI

little tree
little silent Christmas tree
you are so little
you are more like a flower

who found you in the green forest
and were you very sorry to come away?
see   i will comfort you
because you smell so sweetly

i will kiss your cool bark
and hug you safe and tight
just as your mother would,
only don't be afraid

look   the spangles
that sleep all the year in a dark box
dreaming of being taken out and allowed to shine,
the balls the chains red and gold the fluffy threads,

put up your little arms
and i'll give them all to you to hold
every finger shall have its ring
and there won't be a single place dark or unhappy

then when you're quite dressed
you'll stand in the window for everyone to see
and how they'll stare!
oh but you'll be very proud

and my little sister and i will take hands
and looking up at our beautiful tree
we'll dance and sing
"Noel Noel"

E. E. CUMMINGS

The Wind

The wind stood up, and gave a shout;
He whistled on his fingers, and

Kicked the withered leaves about,
And thumped the branches with his hand,

And said he'll kill, and kill, and kill;
And so he will! And so he will!

JAMES STEPHENS

The Sloth

In moving slow he has no Peer.
You ask him something in his ear,
He thinks about it for a Year;

And, then, before he says a Word
There, upside down (unlike a Bird),
He will assume that you have Heard—

A most Ex-as-per-at-ing Lug.
But should you call his manner Smug,
He'll sigh and give his Branch a Hug;

Then off again to Sleep he goes,
Still swaying gently by his Toes,
And you just *know* he knows he knows.

THEODORE ROETHKE

In Praise of a Contented Mind

My mind to me a kingdom is;
   Such perfect joy therein I find
That it excels all other bliss
   That world affords or grows by kind.
Though much I want which most men have,
Yet still my mind forbids to crave.

No princely pomp, no wealthy store,
   No force to win the victory,
No wily wit to salve a sore,
   No shape to feed each gazing eye;
To none of these I yield as thrall.
For why my mind doth serve for all.

I see how plenty suffers oft,
   How hasty climbers soon do fall;
I see that those that are aloft
   Mishap doth threaten most of all;
They get with toil, they keep with fear.
Such cares my mind could never bear.

Content I live, this is my stay;
   I seek no more than may suffice;
I press to bear no haughty sway;
   Look what I lack my mind supplies;
Lo, thus I triumph like a king,
Content with that my mind doth bring.

Some have too much, yet still do crave;
   I little have, and seek no more.
They are but poor, though much they have,
   And I am rich with little store.
They poor, I rich; they beg, I give;
They lack, I leave; they pine, I live.

I laugh not at another's loss;
   I grudge not at another's gain;

No worldly waves my mind can toss;
  My state at one doth still remain.
I fear no foe, nor fawning friend;
I loathe not life, nor dread my end.

Some weigh their pleasure by their lust,
  Their wisdom by their rage of will,
Their treasure is their only trust;
  And cloakéd craft their store of skill.
But all the pleasure that I find
Is to maintain a quiet mind.

My wealth is health and perfect ease;
  My conscience clear my chief defense;
I neither seek by bribes to please,
  Nor by deceit to breed offense.
Thus do I live; thus will I die.
Would all did so as well as I!

ANONYMOUS

Paul Revere's Ride

Listen, my children, and you shall hear
Of the midnight ride of Paul Revere,
On the eighteenth of April, in seventy-five;
Hardly a man is now alive
Who remembers that famous day and year.

He said to his friend, "If the British march
By land or sea from the town tonight,
Hang a lantern aloft in the belfry arch
Of the North Church tower as a signal light,—
One, if by land, and two, if by sea;
And I on the opposite shore will be,
Ready to ride and spread the alarm
Through every Middlesex village and farm,
For the country folk to be up and to arm."
Then he said, "Good night!" and with muffled oar
Silently rowed to the Charlestown shore,
Just as the moon rose over the bay,
Where swinging wide at her moorings lay
The Somerset, British man-of-war;
A phantom ship, with each mast and spar
Across the moon like a prison bar,
And a huge black hulk, that was magnified
By its own reflection in the tide.

Meanwhile, his friend, through alley and street,
Wanders and watches with eager ears,
Till in the silence around him he hears
The muster of men at the barrack door,
The sound of arms, and the tramp of feet,
And the measured tread of the grenadiers,
Marching down to their boats on the shore.

Then he climbed the tower of the Old North Church,
By the wooden stairs, with stealthy tread,
To the belfry-chamber overhead,

And startled the pigeons from their perch
On the somber rafters, that round him made
Masses and moving shapes of shade,—
By the trembling ladder, steep and tall,
To the highest window in the wall,
Where he paused to listen and look down
A moment on the roofs of the town,
And the moonlight flowing over all.

Beneath, in the churchyard, lay the dead,
In their night-encampment on the hill,
Wrapped in silence so deep and still
That he could hear, like a sentinel's tread,
The watchful night-wind, as it went
Creeping along from tent to tent,
And seeming to whisper, "All is well!"
A moment only he feels the spell
Of the place and the hour, and the secret dread
Of the lonely belfry and the dead;
For suddenly all his thoughts are bent
On a shadowy something far away,
Where the river widens to meet the bay,—
A line of black that bends and floats
On the rising tide, like a bridge of boats.

Meanwhile, impatient to mount and ride,
Booted and spurred, with a heavy stride
On the opposite shore walked Paul Revere.
Now he patted his horse's side,
Now gazed at the landscape far and near,
Then, impetuous, stamped the earth,
And turned and tightened his saddle-girth;
But mostly he watched with eager search
The belfry-tower of the Old North Church,
As it rose above the graves on the hill,
Lonely and spectral and somber and still.
And lo! as he looks, on the belfry's height
A glimmer, and then a gleam of light!

He springs to the saddle, the bridle he turns,
But lingers and gazes, till full on his sight
A second lamp in the belfry burns!

A hurry of hoofs in a village street,
A shape in the moonlight, a bulk in the dark,
And beneath, from the pebbles, in passing, a spark
Struck out by a steed flying fearless and fleet:
That was all! And yet, through the gloom and the light,
The fate of a nation was riding that night;
And the spark struck out by that steed, in his flight
Kindled the land into flame with its heat.
He has left the village and mounted the steep,
And beneath him, tranquil and broad and deep,
Is the Mystic, meeting the ocean tides;
And under the alders that skirt its edge,
Now soft on the sand, now loud on the ledge,
Is heard the tramp of his steed as he rides.

It was twelve by the village clock,
When he crossed the bridge into Medford town.
He heard the crowing of the cock,
And the barking of the farmer's dog,
And felt the damp of the river fog,
That rises after the sun goes down.

It was one by the village clock,
When he galloped into Lexington.
He saw the gilded weathercock
Swim in the moonlight as he passed.
And the meeting-house windows, blank and bare,
Gaze at him with a spectral glare,
As if they already stood aghast
At the bloody work they would look upon.

It was two by the village clock,
When he came to the bridge in Concord town.
He heard the bleating of the flock,

And the twitter of birds among the trees,
And felt the breath of the morning breeze
Blowing over the meadows brown.
And one was safe and asleep in his bed
Who at the bridge would be first to fall,
Who that day would be lying dead,
Pierced by a British musket-ball.

You know the rest. In the books you have read,
How the British Regulars fired and fled,—
How the farmers gave them ball for ball,
From behind each fence and farmyard wall,
Chasing the red-coats down the lane,
Then crossing the fields to emerge again
Under the trees at the turn of the road,
And only pausing to fire and load.

So through the night rode Paul Revere;
And so through the night went his cry of alarm
To every Middlesex village and farm,—
A cry of defiance and not of fear,
A voice in the darkness, a knock at the door,
And a word that shall echo forevermore!
For, borne on the night-wind of the Past,
Through all our history, to the last,
In the hour of darkness and peril and need,
The people will waken and listen to hear
The hurrying hoof-beats of that steed,
And the midnight message of Paul Revere.

HENRY WADSWORTH LONGFELLOW

Buffalo Dusk

The buffaloes are gone.
And those who saw the buffaloes are gone.
Those who saw the buffaloes by thousands and how they
pawed the prairie sod into dust with their great hoofs,
their great heads down pawing on in a great pageant
of dusk,
Those who saw the buffaloes are gone.
And the buffaloes are gone.

CARL SANDBURG

The Owl and the Pussy-Cat

The Owl and the Pussy-Cat went to sea
   In a beautiful pea-green boat:
They took some honey, and plenty of money
   Wrapped up in a five-pound note.
The Owl looked up to the stars above,
   And sang to a small guitar,
"O lovely Pussy, O Pussy, my love,
   What a beautiful Pussy you are,
         You are,
         You are!
   What a beautiful Pussy you are!"

Pussy said to the Owl, "You elegant fowl,
   How charmingly sweet you sing!
Oh! let us be married; too long we have tarried!
   But what shall we do for a ring?"
They sailed away, for a year and a day,
   To the land where the bong-tree grows;
And there in a wood a Piggy-wig stood,
   With a ring at the end of his nose,
         His nose,
         His nose,
   With a ring at the end of his nose.

"Dear Pig, are you willing to sell for one shilling
   Your ring?" Said the Piggy, "I will."
So they took it away, and were married next day
   By the turkey who lives on the hill.
They dined on mince and slices of quince,
   Which they ate with a runcible spoon;
And hand in hand, on the edge of the sand,
   They danced by the light of the moon
         The moon,
         The moon,
   They danced by the light of the moon.

EDWARD LEAR

The Eagle

He clasps the crag with crooked hands;
Close to the sun in lonely lands,
Ringed with the azure world, he stands.

The wrinkled sea beneath him crawls;
He watches from his mountain walls,
And like a thunderbolt he falls.

ALFRED, LORD TENNYSON

Roger the Dog

Asleep he wheezes at his ease.
He only wakes to scratch his fleas.

He hogs the fire, he bakes his head
As if it were a loaf of bread.

He's just a sack of snoring dog.
You can lug him like a log.

You can roll him with your foot,
He'll stay snoring where he's put.

I take him out for exercise,
He rolls in cowclap up to his eyes.

He will not race, he will not romp,
He saves his strength for gobble and chomp.

He'll work as hard as you could wish
Emptying his dinner dish,

Then flops flat, and digs down deep,
Like a miner, into sleep.

TED HUGHES

Motherhood

She sat on a shelf,
her breasts two bellies
on her poked-out belly,
on which the navel looked
like a sucked-in mouth—
her knees bent and apart,
her long left arm raised,
with the large hand knuckled
to a bar in the ceiling—
her right hand clamping
the skinny infant to her chest—
its round, pale, new,
soft muzzle hunting
in the brown hair for a nipple,
its splayed, tiny hand picking
at her naked, dirty ear.
Twisting its little neck,
with tortured, ecstatic eyes
the size of lentils, it looked
into her severe, close-set,
solemn eyes, that beneath bald
eyelids glared—dull lights
in sockets of leather.

She twitched some chin-hairs,
with pain or pleasure,
as the baby-mouth found and
yanked at her nipple;
its pink-nailed, jointless
fingers, wandering her face,
tangled in the tufts
of her cliffy brows.

She brought her big
hand down from the bar—
with pretended exasperation
unfastened the little hand,
and locked it within her palm—
while her right hand,
with snag-nailed forefinger
and short, sharp thumb, raked
the new orange hair
of the infant's skinny flank—
and found a louse,
which she lipped, and
thoughtfully crisped
between broad teeth.
She wrinkled appreciative
nostrils, which, without a nose,
stood open—damp, holes
above the poke of her mouth.

She licked her lips, flicked
her leather eyelids—
then, suddenly flung
up both arms and grabbed
the bars overhead.
The baby's scrabbly fingers
instantly caught the hair—
as if there were metal rings there—
in her long, stretched armpits.
And, as she stately swung,
and then proudly, more swiftly
slung herself from corner
to corner of her cell—
arms longer than her round
body, short knees bent—
her little wild-haired,
poke-mouthed infant hung,

like some sort of trophy,
or decoration, or shaggy medal—
shaped like herself—but new,
clean, soft and shining
on her chest.

MAY SWENSON

Bats

A bat is born
Naked and blind and pale.
His mother makes a pocket of her tail
And catches him. He clings to her long fur
By his thumbs and toes and teeth.
And then the mother dances through the night
Doubling and looping, soaring, somersaulting—
Her baby hangs on underneath.
All night, in happiness, she hunts and flies.
Her high sharp cries
Like shining needlepoints of sound
Go out into the night and, echoing back,
Tell her what they have touched.
She hears how far it is, how big it is,
Which way it's going:
She lives by hearing.
The mother eats the moths and gnats she catches
In full flight; in full flight
The mother drinks the water of the pond
She skims across. Her baby hangs on tight.
Her baby drinks the milk she makes him
In moonlight or starlight, in mid-air.
Their single shadow, printed on the moon
Or fluttering across the stars,
Whirls on all night; at daybreak
The tired mother flaps home to her rafter.
The others all are there.
They hang themselves up by their toes,
They wrap themselves in their brown wings.
Bunched upside-down, they sleep in air.
Their sharp ears, their sharp teeth, their quick sharp faces
Are dull and slow and mild.
All the bright day, as the mother sleeps,
She folds her wings about her sleeping child.

RANDALL JARRELL

Narcissa

Some of the girls are playing jacks.
Some are playing ball.
But small Narcissa is not playing
Anything at all.

Small Narcissa sits upon
A brick in her back yard
And looks at tiger lilies,
And shakes her pigtails hard.

First she is an ancient queen
In pomp and purple veil.
Soon she is a singing wind.
And, next, a nightingale.

How fine to be Narcissa,
A-changing like all that!
While sitting still, as still, as still
As anyone ever sat!

GWENDOLYN BROOKS

46

The Cats of Kilkenny

There were once two cats of Kilkenny,
Each thought there was one cat too many;
So they fought and they fit,
And they scratched and they bit,
Till, excepting their nails
And the tips of their tails,
Instead of two cats, there weren't any.

ANONYMOUS

Barbara Frietchie

Up from the meadows rich with corn,
Clear in the cool September morn,

The clustered spires of Frederick stand
Green-walled by the hills of Maryland.

Round about them orchards sweep,
Apple and peach tree fruited deep,

Fair as the garden of the Lord
To the eyes of the famished rebel horde,

On that pleasant morn of the early fall
When Lee marched over the mountain-wall;

Over the mountains winding down,
Horse and foot, into Frederick town.

Forty flags with their silver stars,
Forty flags with their crimson bars,

Flapped in the morning wind: the sun
Of noon looked down, and saw not one.

Up rose old Barbara Frietchie then,
Bowed with her fourscore years and ten;

Bravest of all in Frederick town,
She took up the flag the men hauled down;

In her attic window the staff she set,
To show that one heart was loyal yet.

Up the street came the rebel tread,
Stonewall Jackson riding ahead.

Under his slouched hat left and right
He glanced; the old flag met his sight.

"Halt!"—the dust-brown ranks stood fast.
"Fire!"—out blazed the rifle-blast.

It shivered the window, pane and sash;
It rent the banner with seam and gash.

Quick, as it fell, from the broken staff
Dame Barbara snatched the silken scarf.

She leaned far out on the window-sill,
And shook it forth with a royal will.

"Shoot, if you must, this old gray head,
But spare your country's flag," she said.

A shade of sadness, a blush of shame,
Over the face of the leader came;

The nobler nature within him stirred
To life at that woman's deed and word;

"Who touches a hair of yon gray head
Dies like a dog! March on!" he said.

All day long through Frederick street
Sounded the tread of marching feet:

All day long that free flag tossed
Over the heads of the rebel host.

Ever its torn folds rose and fell
On the loyal winds that loved it well;

And through the hill-gaps sunset light
Shone over it with a warm good-night.

Barbara Frietchie's work is o'er,
And the Rebel rides on his raids no more.

Honor to her! and let a tear
Fall, for her sake, on Stonewall's bier.

Over Barbara Frietchie's grave,
Flag of Freedom and Union, wave!

Peace and order and beauty draw
Round thy symbol of light and law;

And ever the stars above look down
On thy stars below in Frederick town!

JOHN GREENLEAF WHITTIER

The World Is Too Much With Us

The world is too much with us; late and soon,
Getting and spending, we lay waste our powers;
Little we see in Nature that is ours;
We have given our hearts away, a sordid boon!
This Sea that bares her bosom to the moon,
The winds that will be howling at all hours,
And are up-gathered now like sleeping flowers,
For this, for everything, we are out of tune;
It moves us not.—Great God! I'd rather be
A Pagan suckled in a creed outworn;
So might I, standing on this pleasant lea,
Have glimpses that would make me less forlorn;
Have sight of Proteus rising from the sea;
Or hear old Triton blow his wreathéd horn.

WILLIAM WORDSWORTH

O Taste and See

The world is
not with us enough.
O taste and see

the subway Bible poster said,
meaning The Lord, meaning
if anything all that lives
to the imagination's tongue,

grief, mercy, language,
tangerine, weather, to
breathe them, bite,
savor, chew, swallow, transform

into our flesh our
deaths, crossing the street, plum, quince,
living in the orchard and being

hungry, and plucking
the fruit.

DENISE LEVERTOV

O Mistress Mine

O mistress mine, where are you roaming?
O, stay and hear; your true-love's coming,
  That can sing both high and low.
Trip no further, pretty sweeting;
Journeys end in lovers meeting,
  Every wise man's son doth know.

What is love? 'tis not hereafter;
Present mirth hath present laughter;
  What's to come is still unsure.
In delay there lies no plenty;
Then come kiss me, sweet and twenty;
  Youth's a stuff will not endure.

WILLIAM SHAKESPEARE

The Pied Piper of Hamelin; A Child's Story

I

Hamelin Town in Brunswick,
  By famous Hanover city;
The river Weser, deep and wide,
Washes its wall on the southern side;
A pleasanter spot you never spied;
  But, when begins my ditty,
Almost five hundred years ago,
To see the townsfolk suffer so
  From vermin, was a pity.

II

  Rats!
They fought the dogs and killed the cats,
  And bit the babies in the cradles,
And ate the cheeses out of the vats,
  And licked the soup from the cooks' own ladles,
Split open the kegs of salted sprats,
Made nests inside men's Sunday hats,
And even spoiled the women's chats
    By drowning their speaking
    With shrieking and squeaking
In fifty different sharps and flats.

III

At last the people in a body
  To the Town Hall came flocking:
" 'Tis clear," cried they, "our Mayor's a noddy;
  And as for our Corporation—shocking
To think we buy gowns lined with ermine
For dolts that can't or won't determine
What's best to rid us of our vermin!
You hope, because you're old and obese,
To find in the furry civic robe ease?

Rouse up, sirs! Give your brains a racking
To find the remedy we're lacking,
Or, sure as fate, we'll send you packing!"
At this the Mayor and Corporation
Quaked with a mighty consternation.

IV

An hour they sat in council,
    At length the Mayor broke silence:
"For a guilder I'd my ermine gown sell,
    I wish I were a mile hence!
It's easy to bid one rack one's brain—
I'm sure my poor head aches again,
I've scratched it so, and all in vain.
Oh for a trap, a trap, a trap!"
Just as he said this, what should hap
At the chamber door but a gentle tap?
"Bless us," cried the Mayor, "what's that?"
(With the Corporation as he sat,
Looking little though wondrous fat;
Nor brighter was his eye, nor moister
Than a too-long-opened oyster,
Save when at noon his paunch grew mutinous
For a plate of turtle, green and glutinous)
"Only a scraping of shoes on the mat?
Anything like the sound of a rat
Makes my heart go pit-a-pat!"

V

"Come in!" the Mayor cried, looking bigger:
And in did come the strangest figure!
His queer long coat from heel to head
Was half of yellow and half of red,
And he himself was tall and thin,
With sharp blue eyes, each like a pin,
And light loose hair, yet swarthy skin,
No tuft on cheek nor beard on chin,

But lips where smiles went out and in;
There was no guessing his kith and kin:
And nobody could enough admire
The tall man and his quaint attire.
Quoth one: "It's as my great-grandsire,
Starting up at the Trump of Doom's tone,
Had walked this way from his painted
    tombstone!"

VI

He advanced to the council-table:
And, "Please your honors," said he, "I'm able,
By means of a secret charm, to draw
    All creatures living beneath the sun,
    That creep or swim or fly or run,
After me so as you never saw!
And I chiefly use my charm
On creatures that do people harm,
The mole and toad and newt and viper;
And people call me the Pied Piper."
(And here they noticed round his neck
    A scarf of red and yellow stripe,
To match with his coat of the self-same check;
    And at the scarf's end hung a pipe;
And his fingers, they noticed, were ever straying
As if impatient to be playing
Upon this pipe, as low it dangled
Over his vesture so old-fangled.)
"Yet," said he, "poor piper as I am,
In Tartary I freed the Cham,
    Last June, from his huge swarms of gnats;
I eased in Asia the Nizam
    Of a monstrous brood of vampire-bats:
And as for what your brain bewilders,
    If I can rid your town of rats
Will you give me a thousand guilders?"

"One? fifty thousand!"—was the exclamation
Of the astonished Mayor and Corporation.

VII

Into the street the Piper stepped,
   Smiling first a little smile,
As if he knew what magic slept
   In his quiet pipe the while;
Then, like a musical adept,
To blow the pipe his lips he wrinkled,
And green and blue his sharp eyes twinkled,
Like a candle-flame where salt is sprinkled;
And ere three shrill notes the pipe uttered,
You heard as if an army muttered;
And the muttering grew to a grumbling;
And the grumbling grew to a mighty rumbling;
And out of the houses the rats came tumbling.
Great rats, small rats, lean rats, brawny rats,
Brown rats, black rats, gray rats, tawny rats,
Grave old plodders, gay young friskers,
   Fathers, mothers, uncles, cousins,
Cocking tails and pricking whiskers,
   Families by tens and dozens,
Brothers, sisters, husbands, wives—
Followed the Piper for their lives.
From street to street he piped advancing,
And step for step they followed dancing,
Until they came to the river Weser,
   Wherein all plunged and perished!
—Save one who, stout as Julius Caesar,
Swam across and lived to carry
   (As he, the manuscript he cherished)
To Rat-land home his commentary:
Which was, "At the first shrill notes of the pipe,
I heard a sound as of scraping tripe,
And putting apples, wondrous ripe,
Into a cider-press's gripe:

And a moving away of pickle-tub-boards,
And a leaving ajar of conserve-cupboards,
And a drawing the corks of train-oil-flasks,
And a breaking the hoops of butter-casks;
And it seemed as if a voice
   (Sweeter far than bý harp or bý psaltery
Is breathed) called out, 'Oh rats, rejoice!
   The world is grown to one vast drysaltery!
So munch on, crunch on, take your nuncheon,
Breakfast, supper, dinner, luncheon!'
And just as a bulky sugar-puncheon,
All ready staved, like a great sun shone
Glorious scarce an inch before me,
Just as methought it said, 'Come, bore me!'
—I found the Weser rolling o'er me."

VIII

You should have heard the Hamelin people
Ringing the bells till they rocked the steeple.
"Go," cried the Mayor, "and get long poles,
Poke out the nests and block up the holes!
Consult with carpenters and builders,
And leave in our town not even a trace
Of the rats!"—when suddenly, up the face
Of the Piper perked in the market-place,
With a "First, if you please, my thousand
    guilders!"

IX

A thousand guilders! The Mayor looked blue;
So did the Corporation too.
For council dinners made rare havoc
With Claret, Moselle, Vin-de-Grave, Hock;
And half the money would replenish
Their cellar's biggest butt with Rhenish.
To pay this sum to a wandering fellow
With a gypsy coat of red and yellow!

"Beside," quoth the Mayor with a knowing wink,
"Our business was done at the river's brink;
We saw with our eyes the vermin sink,
And what's dead can't come to life, I think.
So, friend, we're not the folks to shrink
From the duty of giving you something for drink,
And a matter of money to put in your poke;
But as for the guilders, what we spoke
Of them, as you very well know, was in joke.
Besides, our losses have made us thrifty.
A thousand guilders! Come, take fifty!"

X

The Piper's face fell, and he cried
"No trifling! I can't wait, beside!
I've promised to visit by dinnertime
Baghdad, and accept the prime
Of the Head-Cook's pottage, all he's rich in,
For having left, in the Caliph's kitchen,
Of a nest of scorpions no survivor:
With him I proved no bargain-driver,
With you, don't think I'll bate a stiver!
And folks who put me in a passion
May find me pipe after another fashion."

XI

"How?" cried the Mayor, "d'ye think I brook
Being worse treated than a cook?
Insulted by a lazy ribald
With idle pipe and vesture piebald?
You threaten us, fellow? Do your worst,
Blow your pipe there till you burst!"

XII

Once more he stepped into the street
    And to his lips again
    Laid his long pipe of smooth straight cane;

And ere he blew three notes (such sweet
Soft notes as yet musician's cunning
   Never gave the enraptured air)
There was a rustling that seemed like a bustling
Of merry crowds justling at pitching and hustling
Small feet were pattering, wooden shoes clattering,
Little hands clapping and little tongues chattering,
And, like fowls in a farmyard when barley is scattering,
Out came the children running.
All the little boys and girls,
With rosy cheeks and flaxen curls,
And sparkling eyes and teeth like pearls,
Tripping and skipping, ran merrily after
The wonderful music with shouting and laughter.

XIII

The Mayor was dumb, and the Council stood
As if they were changed into blocks of wood,
Unable to move a step, or cry
To the children merrily skipping by
—Could only follow with the eye
That joyous crowd at the Piper's back.
But how the Mayor was on the rack,
And the wretched Council's bosoms beat,
As the Piper turned from the High Street
To where the Weser rolled its waters
Right in the way of their sons and daughters!
However he turned from south to west,
And to Koppelberg Hill his steps addressed,
And after him the children pressed;
Great was the joy in every breast.
"He never can cross that mighty top!
He's forced to let the piping drop,
And we shall see our children stop!"
When, lo, as they reached the mountain-side,
A wondrous portal opened wide,
As if a cavern was suddenly hollowed;

And the Piper advanced and the children followed,
And when all were in to the very last,
The door in the mountain-side shut fast.
Did I say, all? No! One was lame,
    And could not dance the whole of the way;
And in after years, if you would blame
    His sadness, he was used to say—
"It's dull in our town since my playmates left!
I can't forget that I'm bereft
Of all the pleasant sights they see,
Which the Piper also promised me.
For he led us, he said, to a joyous land,
Joining the town and just at hand,
Where waters gushed and fruit trees grew
And flowers put forth a fairer hue,
And everything was strange and new;
The sparrows were brighter than peacocks here,
And their dogs outran our fallow deer,
And honey-bees had lost their stings,
And horses were born with eagles' wings:
And just as I became assured
My lame foot would be speedily cured,
The music stopped and I stood still,
And found myself outside the hill,
Left alone against my will,
To go now limping as before,
And never hear of that country more!"

XIV

Alas, alas for Hamelin!
    There came into many a burgher's pate
    A text which says that heaven's gate
    Opes to the rich at as easy rate
As the needle's eye takes a camel in!
The Mayor sent east, west, north, and south,
To offer the Piper, by word of mouth,
    Wherever it was men's lot to find him,

Silver and gold to his heart's content,
If he'd only return the way he went,
　　And bring the children behind him.
But when they saw 'twas a lost endeavor,
And Piper and dancers were gone for ever,
They made a decree that lawyers never
　　Should think their records dated duly
If, after the day of the month and year,
These words did not as well appear,
"And so long after what happened here
　　On the Twenty-second of July,
Thirteen hundred and seventy-six";
And the better in memory to fix
The place of the children's last retreat,
They called it the Pied Piper's Street—
Where anyone playing on pipe or tabor
Was sure for the future to lose his labor.
Nor suffered they hostelry or tavern
　　To shock with mirth a street so solemn;
But opposite the place of the cavern
　　They wrote the story on a column;
And on the great church-window painted
The same, to make the world acquainted
How their children were stolen away,
And there it stands to this very day.
And I must not omit to say
That in Transylvania there's a tribe
Of alien people who ascribe
The outlandish ways and dress
On which their neighbors lay such stress,
To their fathers and mothers having risen
Out of some subterraneous prison
Into which they were trepanned
Long time ago in a mighty band
Out of Hamelin town in Brunswick land,
But how or why, they don't understand.

XV

So, Willy, let you and me be wipers
Of scores out with all men—especially pipers!
And, whether they pipe us free from rats or from mice,
If we've promised them aught, let us keep our promise!

ROBERT BROWNING

Against Idleness and Mischief

How doth the little busy bee
  Improve each shining hour,
And gather honey all the day
  From every opening flower!

How skillfully she builds her cell!
  How neat she spreads the wax!
And labors hard to store it well
  With the sweet food she makes.

In works of labor or of skill,
  I would be busy too;
For Satan finds some mischief still
  For idle hands to do.

In books, or work, or healthful play,
  Let my first years be passed,
That I may give for every day
  Some good account at last.

ISAAC WATTS

Emily Jane

Oh! Christmas time is coming again,
And what shall I buy for Emily Jane?
O Emily Jane, my love so true,
Now what upon earth shall I buy for you?
My Emily Jane, my doll so dear,
I've loved you now for many a year,
And still while there's anything left of you,
My Emily Jane, I'll love you true!

My Emily Jane has lost her head,
And has a potato tied on instead;
A hole for an eye, and a lump for a nose,
It really looks better than you would suppose.
My Emily Jane has lost her arms,
The half of one leg's the extent of her charms;
But still, while there's anything left of you,
My Emily Jane, I'll love you true.

And now, shall I bring you a fine new head,
Or shall I bring you a leg instead?
Or will you have arms, to hug me tight,
When naughty 'Lizabeth calls you a fright?
Or I'll buy you a dress of satin so fine,
'Mong all the dolls to shimmer and shine;
For oh! while there's anything left of you,
My Emily Jane, I'll love you true!

Mamma says, "Keep all your pennies, Sue,
And I'll buy you a doll all whole and new."
But better I love my dear old doll,
With her one half-leg and potato poll.
"The potato may rot, and the leg may fall?"
Well, then I shall treasure the sawdust, that's all!
For while there is *anything* left of you,
My Emily Jane, I'll love you true!

LAURA E. RICHARDS

Annabel Lee

It was many and many a year ago,
    In a kingdom by the sea,
That a maiden there lived whom you may know
    By the name of Annabel Lee;
And this maiden she lived with no other thought
    Than to love and be loved by me.

She was a child and *I* was a child,
    In this kingdom by the sea,
But we loved with a love that was more than love—
    I and my Annabel Lee—
With a love that the wingéd seraphs of Heaven
    Coveted her and me.

And this was the reason that, long ago,
    In this kingdom by the sea,
A wind blew out of a cloud by night
    Chilling my Annabel Lee;
So that her highborn kinsmen came
    And bore her away from me,
To shut her up in a sepulchre
    In this kingdom by the sea.

The angels, not half so happy in Heaven,
    Went envying her and me:
Yes! that was the reason (as all men know,
    In this kingdom by the sea)
That the wind came out of the cloud, chilling
    And killing my Annabel Lee.

But our love it was stronger by far than the love
    Of those who were older than we—
    Of many far wiser than we—
And neither the angels in Heaven above
    Nor the demons down under the sea,
Can ever dissever my soul from the soul
    Of the beautiful Annabel Lee:

For the moon never beams without bringing me dreams
　　Of the beautiful Annabel Lee;
And the stars never rise but I see the bright eyes
　　Of the beautiful Annabel Lee;
And so, all the night-tide, I lie down by the side
Of my darling, my darling, my life and my bride,
　　In her sepulchre there by the sea—
　　In her tomb by the side of the sea.

EDGAR ALLAN POE

since feeling is first
who pays any attention
to the syntax of things
will never wholly kiss you;

wholly to be a fool
while Spring is in the world

my blood approves,
and kisses are a better fate
than wisdom
lady i swear by all flowers. Don't cry
—the best gesture of my brain is less than
your eyelids' flutter which says

we are for each other: then
laugh, leaning back in my arms
for life's not a paragraph

And death i think is no parenthesis

E. E. CUMMINGS

In These
Dissenting Times

*To acknowledge our ancestors means we are
aware that we did not make ourselves, that the line
stretches all the way back, perhaps, to God; or to
Gods. We remember them because it is an easy
thing to forget: that we are not the first to suffer,
rebel, fight, love and die. The grace with which we
embrace life, in spite of the pain, the sorrows, is
always a measure of what has gone before.*
—Alice Walker, "Fundamental Difference"

IN THESE DISSENTING TIMES

I shall write of the old men I knew
And the young men
I loved
And of the gold toothed women
Mighty of arm
Who dragged us all
To church.

1

THE OLD MEN USED TO SING

The old men used to sing
And lifted a brother
Carefully
Out the door
I used to think they
Were born
Knowing how to
Gently swing
A casket
They shuffled softly
Eyes dry
     More awkward
With the flowers
Than with the widow

After they'd put the
Body in
And stood around waiting
In their
Brown suits.

2

WINKING AT A FUNERAL

Those were the days
Of winking at a
Funeral
Romance blossomed
In the pews
Love signaled
Through the
Hymns
What did we know?

Who smelled the flowers
Slowly fading
Knew the arsonist
Of the church?

3

WOMEN

They were women then
My mama's generation
Husky of voice—Stout of
Step
With fists as well as
Hands
How they battered down
Doors
And ironed
Starched white
Shirts
How they led
Armies

Headragged Generals
Across mined
Fields
Booby-trapped
Ditches
To discover books
Desks
A place for us
How they knew what we
Must know
Without knowing a page
Of it
Themselves.

4

THREE DOLLARS CASH

Three dollars cash
For a pair of catalog shoes
Was what the midwife charged
My mama
For bringing me.
"We wasn't so country then," says Mom,
"You being the last one—
And we couldn't, like
We done
When she brought your
Brother,
Send her out to the
Pen
And let her pick
Out
A pig."

5

YOU HAD TO GO TO FUNERALS

You had to go to funerals
Even if you didn't know the
People

Your Mama always did
Usually your Pa.
In new patent leather shoes
It wasn't so bad
And if it rained
The graves dropped open
And if the sun was shining
You could take some of the
Flowers home
In your pocket
book. At six and seven
The face in the gray box
Is always your daddy's
Old schoolmate
Mowed down before his
Time.
You don't even ask
After a while
What makes them lie so
Awfully straight
And still. If there's a picture of
Jesus underneath
The coffin lid
You might, during a boring sermon,
Without shouting or anything,
Wonder who painted it;

And how *he* would like
All eternity to stare
It down.

6

UNCLES

They had broken teeth
And billy club scars
But we didn't notice
Or mind

They were uncles.
It was their *job*
To come home every summer
From the North
And tell my father
He wasn't no man
And make my mother
Cry and long
For Denver, Jersey City,
Philadelphia.
They were uncles.
Who noticed how
Much
They drank
And acted womanish
With they do-rags
We were nieces.
And they were almost
Always good
For a nickel
Sometimes
a dime.

7

THEY TAKE A LITTLE NIP

They take a little nip
Now and then
Do the old folks
Now they've moved to
Town
You'll sometimes
See them sitting
Side by side
On the porch

Straightly
As in church

Or working diligently
Their small
City stand of
Greens

Serenely pulling
Stalks and branches
Up
Leaving all
The weeds.

8

SUNDAY SCHOOL, CIRCA 1950

"Who made you?" was always
The question
The answer was always
"God."   .
Well, there we stood
Three feet high
Heads bowed
Leaning into
Bosoms.

Now
I no longer recall
The Catechism
Or brood on the Genesis
Of life
No.

I ponder the exchange
Itself
And salvage mostly
The leaning.

ALICE WALKER

Fireflies in the Garden

Here come real stars to fill the upper skies,
And here on earth come emulating flies
That, though they never equal stars in size
(And they were never really stars at heart),
Achieve at times a very starlike start.
Only, of course, they can't sustain the part.

ROBERT FROST

John Smith and his son, John Smith,
  And his son's son John, and-a-one
  And-a-two and-a-three
And-a-rum-tum-tum, and-a
Lean John, and his son, lean John,
  And his lean son's John, and-a-one
  And-a-two and-a-three
And-a-drum-rum-rum, and-a
Rich John, and his son, rich John,
  And his rich son's John, and-a-one
  And-a-two and-a-three
And-a-pom-pom-pom, and-a
Wise John, and his son, wise John,
  And his wise son's John, and-a-one
  And-a-two and-a-three
And-a-fee and-a-fee and-a-fee
  And-a-fee-fo-fum—
Voilà la vie, la vie, la vie,
  And-a-rummy-tummy-tum
  And-a-rummy-tummy-tum.

WALLACE STEVENS

The Flattered Flying Fish

Said the Shark to the Flying Fish over the phone:
"Will you join me tonight? I am dining alone.
Let me order a nice little dinner for two!
And come as you are, in your shimmering blue."

Said the Flying Fish: "Fancy remembering me,
And the dress that I wore at the Porpoises' tea!"
"How could I forget?" said the Shark in his guile:
"I expect you at eight!" and rang off with a smile.

She has powdered her nose; she has put on her things;
She is off with one flap of her luminous wings.
O little one, lovely, light-hearted and vain,
The Moon will not shine on your beauty again!

E. V. RIEU

Snake

A snake came to my water-trough
On a hot, hot day, and I in pajamas for the heat,
To drink there.

In the deep, strange-scented shade of the great dark carob-tree
I came down the steps with my pitcher
And must wait, must stand and wait, for there he was at the
    trough before me.

He reached down from a fissure in the earth-wall in the gloom
And trailed his yellow-brown slackness soft-bellied down, over
    the edge of the stone trough
And rested his throat upon the stone bottom,
And where the water had dripped from the tap, in a small
    clearness,
He sipped with his straight mouth,
Softly drank through his straight gums, into his slack long body,
Silently.

Someone was before me at my water-trough,
And I, like a second comer, waiting.

He lifted his head from his drinking, as cattle do,
And looked at me vaguely, as drinking cattle do,
And flickered his two-forked tongue from his lips, and mused a
    moment,
And stooped and drank a little more,
Being earth-brown, earth-golden from the burning bowels of the
    earth
On the day of Sicilian July, with Etna smoking.

The voice of my education said to me
He must be killed,
For in Sicily the black, black snakes are innocent, the gold are
    venomous.

And voices in me said, If you were a man

You would take a stick and break him now, and finish him off.

But must I confess how I liked him,
How glad I was he had come like a guest in quiet, to drink at
    my water-trough
And depart peaceful, pacified, and thankless,
Into the burning bowels of this earth?

Was it cowardice, that I dared not kill him?
Was it perversity, that I longed to talk to him?
Was it humility, to feel so honored?
I felt so honored.

And yet those voices:
If you were not afraid, you would kill him!

And truly I was afraid, I was most afraid,
But even so, honored still more
That he should seek my hospitality
From out the dark door of the secret earth.

He drank enough
And lifted his head, dreamily, as one who has drunken,
And flickered his tongue like a forked night on the air, so black,
Seeming to lick his lips,
And looked around like a god, unseeing, into the air,
And slowly turned his head,
And slowly, very slowly, as if thrice adream,
Proceeded to draw his slow length curving round
And climb again the broken bank of my wall-face.

And as he put his head into that dreadful hole,
And as he slowly drew up, snake-easing his shoulders, and
    entered farther,
A sort of horror, a sort of protest against his withdrawing into
    that horrid black hole,
Deliberately going into the blackness, and slowly drawing
    himself after,
Overcame me now his back was turned.

I looked round, I put down my pitcher,
I picked up a clumsy log
And threw it at the water-trough with a clatter.

I think it did not hit him,
But suddenly that part of him that was left behind convulsed in
    undignified haste,
Writhed like lightning, and was gone
Into the black hole, the earth-lipped fissure in the wall-front,
At which, in the intense still noon, I stared with fascination.

And immediately I regretted it.
I thought how paltry, how vulgar, what a mean act!
I despised myself and the voices of my accursed human
    education.

And I thought of the albatross,
And I wished he would come back, my snake.

For he seemed to me again like a king,
Like a king in exile, uncrowned in the underworld,
Now due to be crowned again.

And so, I missed my chance with one of the lords
Of life.
And I have something to expiate;
A pettiness.

D. H. LAWRENCE

April Rain Song

Let the rain kiss you.
Let the rain beat upon your head with silver liquid drops.
Let the rain sing you a lullaby.

The rain makes still pools on the sidewalk.
The rain makes running pools in the gutter.
The rain plays a little sleep-song on our roof at night—

And I love the rain.

LANGSTON HUGHES

Hay for the Horses

He had driven half the night
From far down San Joaquin
Through Mariposa, up the
Dangerous mountain roads,
And pulled in at eight a.m.,
With his big truckload of hay behind the barn.
With winch and ropes and hooks
We stacked the bales up clean
To splintery redwood rafters
High in the dark, flecks of alfalfa
Whirling through shingle-cracks of light,
Itch of haydust in the sweaty shirt and shoes.
At lunchtime under black oak
Out in the hot corral,
—The old mare nosing lunchpails,
Grasshoppers crackling in the weeds—
"I'm sixty-eight" he said,
"I first bucked hay when I was seventeen.
I thought, that day I started,
I sure would hate to do this all my life.
And dammit, that's just what
I've gone and done."

GARY SNYDER

The Walrus and the Carpenter

The sun was shining on the sea,
  Shining with all his might;
He did his very best to make
  The billows smooth and bright—
And this was odd, because it was
  The middle of the night.

The moon was shining sulkily,
  Because she thought the sun
Had got no business to be there
  After the day was done—
"It's very rude of him," she said,
  "To come and spoil the fun!"

The sea was wet as wet could be,
  The sands were dry as dry.
You could not see a cloud, because
  No cloud was in the sky;
No birds were flying overhead—
  There were no birds to fly.

The Walrus and the Carpenter
  Were walking close at hand;
They wept like anything to see
  Such quantities of sand.
"If this were only cleared away,"
  They said, "it *would* be grand!"

"If seven maids with seven mops
  Swept it for half a year,
Do you suppose," the Walrus said,
  "That they could get it clear?"
"I doubt it," said the Carpenter,
  And shed a bitter tear.

"O Oysters, come and walk with us!"
  The Walrus did beseech.

"A pleasant walk, a pleasant talk,
    Along the briny beach;
We cannot do with more than four,
    To give a hand to each."

The eldest Oyster looked at him,
    But never a word he said;
The eldest Oyster winked his eye,
    And shook his heavy head—
Meaning to say he did not choose
    To leave the oyster-bed.

But four young Oysters hurried up,
    All eager for the treat;
Their coats were brushed, their faces washed,
    Their shoes were clean and neat—
And this was odd, because, you know,
    They hadn't any feet.

Four other Oysters followed them,
    And yet another four;
And thick and fast they came at last,
    And more, and more, and more—
All hopping through the frothy waves,
    And scrambling to the shore.

The Walrus and the Carpenter
    Walked on a mile or so,
And then they rested on a rock
    Conveniently low;
And all the little Oysters stood
    And waited in a row.

"The time has come," the Walrus said,
    "To talk of many things:
Of shoes—and ships—and sealing-wax—
    Of cabbages—and kings—
And why the sea is boiling hot—
    And whether pigs have wings."

"But wait a bit," the Oysters cried,
    "Before we have our chat;
For some of us are out of breath,
    And all of us are fat!"
"No hurry!" said the Carpenter.
    They thanked him much for that.

"A loaf of bread," the Walrus said,
    "Is what we chiefly need;
Pepper and vinegar besides
    Are very good indeed—
Now, if you're ready, Oysters dear,
    We can begin to feed."

"But not on us!" the Oysters cried,
    Turning a little blue.
"After such kindness, that would be
    A dismal thing to do!"
"The night is fine," the Walrus said,
    "Do you admire the view?

"It was so kind of you to come!
    And you are very nice!"
The Carpenter said nothing but
    "Cut us another slice.
I wish you were not quite so deaf—
    I've had to ask you twice!"

"It seems a shame," the Walrus said,
    "To play them such a trick,
After we've brought them out so far,
    And made them trot so quick!"
The Carpenter said nothing but
    "The butter's spread too thick!"

"I weep for you," the Walrus said;
    "I deeply sympathize."
With sobs and tears he sorted out
    Those of the largest size,

Holding his pocket-handkerchief
  Before his streaming eyes.

"O Oysters," said the Carpenter,
  "You've had a pleasant run!
Shall we be trotting home again?"
  But answer came there none—
And this was scarcely odd, because
  They'd eaten every one.

LEWIS CARROLL

God moves in a mysterious way,
  His wonders to perform;
He plants his footsteps in the sea,
  And rides upon the storm.

Deep in unfathomable mines
  Of never failing skill;
He treasures up his bright designs,
  And works his sovereign will.

Ye fearful saints fresh courage take,
  The clouds ye so much dread
Are big with mercy, and shall break
  In blessings on your head.

Judge not the Lord by feeble sense,
  But trust him for his grace;
Behind a frowning providence,
  He hides a smiling face.

His purposes will ripen fast,
  Unfolding ev'ry hour;
The bud may have a bitter taste,
  But sweet will be the flow'r.

Blind unbelief is sure to err,
  And scan his work in vain;
God is his own interpreter,
  And he will make it plain.

WILLIAM COWPER

Hymn to Cynthia

Queen and huntress, chaste and fair,
Now the sun is laid to sleep,
Seated in thy silver chair,
State in wonted manner keep.
 Hesperus entreats thy light,
 Goddess excellently bright.

Earth, let not thy envious shade
Dare itself to interpose;
Cynthia's shining orb was made
Heaven to clear, when day did close.
 Bless us then with wishèd sight,
 Goddess excellently bright.

Lay thy bow of pearl apart,
And thy crystal-shining quiver;
Give unto the flying hart
Space to breathe, how short soever;
 Thou that mak'st a day of night,
 Goddess excellently bright.

BEN JONSON

Ballad of Birmingham

(On the bombing of a church in Birmingham, Alabama, 1963)

"Mother dear, may I go downtown
Instead of out to play,
And march the streets of Birmingham
In a Freedom March today?"

"No, baby, no, you may not go,
For the dogs are fierce and wild,
And clubs and hoses, guns and jails
Aren't good for a little child."

"But, mother, I won't be alone.
Other children will go with me,
And march the streets of Birmingham
To make our country free."

"No, baby, no, you may not go,
For I fear those guns will fire.
But you may go to church instead
And sing in the children's choir."

She has combed and brushed her night-dark hair,
And bathed rose petal sweet,
And drawn white gloves on her small brown hands,
And white shoes on her feet.

The mother smiled to know her child
Was in the sacred place,
But that smile was the last smile
To come upon her face.

For when she heard the explosion,
Her eyes grew wet and wild.
She raced through the streets of Birmingham
Calling for her child.

She clawed through bits of glass and brick,
Then lifted out a shoe.
"O, here's the shoe my baby wore,
But, baby, where are you?"

DUDLEY RANDALL

Ducks' Ditty

All along the backwater,
Through the rushes tall,
Ducks are a-dabbling.
Up tails all!

Ducks' tails, drakes' tails,
Yellow feet a-quiver,
Yellow bills all out of sight
Busy in the river!

Slushy green undergrowth
Where the roach swim—
Here we keep our larder,
Cool and full and dim.

Every one for what he likes!
We like to be
Head down, tails up,
Dabbling free!

High in the blue above
Swifts whirl and call—
We are down a-dabbling
Up tails all!

KENNETH GRAHAME

November Calf

She calved in the ravine, beside
the green-scummed pond.
Full clouds and mist hung low—
it was unseasonably warm. Steam
rose from her head as she pushed
and called; her cries went out
over the still-lush fields.

First came the front feet, then
the blossom-nose, shell-pink
and glistening; and then the broad
forehead, flopping black ears,
and neck. . . . She worked
until the steaming length of him
rushed out onto the ground, then
turned and licked him with her wide
pink tongue. He lifted up his head
and looked around.

The herd pressed close to see, then
frolicked up the bank, flicking
their tails. It looked like revelry.
The farmer set off for the barn,
swinging in a widening arc
a frayed and knotted scrap of rope.

JANE KENYON

My Heart Leaps Up

My heart leaps up when I behold
  A rainbow in the sky:
So was it when my life began;
So is it now I am a man;
So be it when I shall grow old,
  Or let me die!
The Child is father of the Man;
And I could wish my days to be
Bound each to each by natural piety.

WILLIAM WORDSWORTH

The Vulture

The Vulture eats between his meals,
   And that's the reason why
He very, very rarely feels
   As well as you and I.

His eye is dull, his head is bald,
   His neck is growing thinner.
Oh! what a lesson for us all
   To only eat at dinner!

HILAIRE BELLOC

The Deacon's Masterpiece

Or, the Wonderful "One-Hoss Shay"

A LOGICAL STORY

Have you heard of the wonderful one-hoss shay,
That was built in such a logical way
It ran a hundred years to a day,
And then, of a sudden, it—ah, but stay,
I'll tell you what happened without delay,
Scaring the parson into fits,
Frightening people out of their wits,—
Have you ever heard of that, I say?

Seventeen hundred and fifty-five.
Georgius Secundus was then alive,—
Snuffy old drone from the German hive.
That was the year when Lisbon-town
Saw the earth open and gulp her down,
And Braddock's army was done so brown,
Left without a scalp to its crown.
It was on the terrible Earthquake-day
That the Deacon finished the one-hoss shay.

Now in building of chaises, I tell you what,
There is always *somewhere* a weakest spot,—
In hub, tire, felloe, in spring or thill,
In panel, or crossbar, or floor, or sill,
In screw, bolt, thoroughbrace,—lurking still,
Find it somewhere you must and will,—
Above or below, or within or without—
And that's the reason, beyond a doubt,
That a chaise *breaks down*, but doesn't *wear out*.

But the Deacon swore (as Deacons do,
With an "I dew vum," or an "I tell *yeou*,")
He would build one shay to beat the taown
'n' the keounty 'n' all the kentry raoun';
It should be so built that it *couldn'* break daown:

95

—"Fur," said the Deacon, " 't's mighty plain
Thut the weakes' place mus' stan' the strain;
'n' the way t' fix it, uz I maintain,
                    Is only jest
T'make that place uz strong uz the rest."

So the Deacon inquired of the village folk
Where he could find the strongest oak,
That couldn't be split nor bent nor broke,—
That was for spokes and floor and sills;
.He sent for lancewood to make the thills;
The crossbars were ash, from the straightest trees,
The panels of white-wood, that cuts like cheese,
But lasts like iron for things like these;
The hubs of logs from the "Settler's ellum,"—
Last of its timber,—they couldn't sell 'em,
Never an ax had seen their chips,
And the wedges flew from between their lips,
Their blunt ends frizzled like celery-tips;
Step and prop-iron, bolt and screw,
Spring, tire, axle, and linchpin too,
Steel of the finest, bright and blue;
Thoroughbrace bison-skin, thick and wide;
Boot, top, dasher, from tough old hide
Found in the pit when the tanner died.
That was the way he "put her through."—
"There!" said the Deacon, "naow she'll dew!"

Do! I tell you, I rather guess
She was a wonder, and nothing less!
Colts grew horses, beards turned gray,
Deacon and deaconess dropped away,
Children and grandchildren—where were they?
But there stood the stout old one-hoss shay
As fresh as on Lisbon-earthquake-day!

Eighteen hundred;—it came and found
The Deacon's masterpiece strong and sound.

Eighteen hundred increased by ten;—
"Hahnsum kerridge" they called it then.
Eighteen hundred and twenty came;—
Running as usual; much the same.
Thirty and forty at last arrive,
And then come fifty, and fifty-five.

Little of all we value here
Wakes on the morn of its hundredth year
Without both feeling and looking queer.
In fact, there's nothing that keeps its youth,
So far as I know, but a tree and truth.
(This is a moral that runs at large;
Take it.—You're welcome.—No extra charge.)

First of November,—the Earthquake-day—
There are traces of age in the one-hoss shay,
A general flavor of mild decay,
But nothing local, as one may say.
There couldn't be,—for the Deacon's art
Had made it so like in every part
That there wasn't a chance for one to start.
For the wheels were just as strong as the thills,
And the floor was just as strong as the sills,
And the panels just as strong as the floor,
And the whipple-tree neither less nor more,
And the back-crossbar as strong as the fore,
And spring and axle and hub *encore*.
And yet, *as a whole*, it is past a doubt
In another hour it will be *worn out*!

First of November, 'Fifty-five!
This morning the parson takes a drive.
Now, small boys, get out of the way!
Here comes the wonderful one-hoss shay,
Drawn by a rat-tailed, ewe-necked bay.
"Huddup!" said the parson.—Off went they.

The parson was working his Sunday's text,—
Had got to *fifthly*, and stopped perplexed
At what the—Moses!—was coming next.
All at once the horse stood still,
Close by the meet'n'-house on the hill.
—First a shiver, and then a thrill,
Then something decidedly like a spill,—
And the parson was sitting upon a rock,
At half-past nine by the meet'n'-house clock.
Just the hour of the Earthquake shock!
—What do you think the parson found,
When he got up and stared around?
The poor old chaise in a heap or mound,
As if it had been to the mill and ground!
You see, of course, if you're not a dunce,
How it went to pieces all at once—
All at once, and nothing first—
Just as bubbles do when they burst.

End of the wonderful one-hoss shay.
Logic is logic. That's all I say.

OLIVER WENDELL HOLMES

Loving You Less Than Life, a Little Less

Loving you less than life, a little less
Than bitter-sweet upon a broken wall
Or brush-wood smoke in autumn, I confess
I cannot swear I love you not at all.
For there is that about you in this light—
A yellow darkness, sinister of rain—
Which sturdily recalls my stubborn sight
To dwell on you, and dwell on you again.
And I am made aware of many a week
I shall consume, remembering in what way
Your brown hair grows about your brow and cheek,
And what divine absurdities you say:
Till all the world, and I, and surely you,
Will know I love you, whether or not I do.

EDNA ST. VINCENT MILLAY

maggie and millie and molly and may
went down to the beach(to play one day)

and maggie discovered a shell that sang
so sweetly she couldn't remember her troubles,and

milly befriended a stranded star
whose rays five languid fingers were;

and molly was chased by a horrible thing
which raced sideways while blowing bubbles:and

may came home with a smooth round stone
as small as a world and as large as alone.

For whatever we lost(like a you or a me)
it's always ourselves we find in the sea

E. E. CUMMINGS

The Sluggard

'Tis the voice of a sluggard; I heard him complain—
"You have waked me too soon; I must slumber again;"
As the door on its hinges, so he on his bed,
Turns his sides, and his shoulders, and his heavy head.

"A little more sleep, and a little more slumber"—
Thus he wastes half his days, and his hours without number;
And when he gets up, he sits folding his hands,
Or walks about saunt'ring, or trifling he stands.

I passed by his garden, and saw the wild brier,
The thorn and the thistle grow broader and higher;
The clothes that hang on him are turning to rags;
And his money still wastes till he starves or he begs.

I made him a visit, still hoping to find
That he took better care for improving his mind:
He told me his dreams, talked of eating and drinking,
But he scarce reads his Bible, and never loves thinking.

Said I then to my heart: "Here's a lesson for me;
That man's but a picture of what I might be;
But thanks to my friends for their care in my breeding,
Who taught me betimes to love working and reading."

ISAAC WATTS

We Are Seven

——A simple child,
That lightly draws its breath,
And feels its life in every limb,
What should it know of death?

I met a little cottage girl:
She was eight years old, she said;
Her hair was thick with many a curl
That clustered round her head.

She had a rustic, woodland air,
And she was wildly clad:
Her eyes were fair, and very fair;
——Her beauty made me glad.

"Sisters and brothers, little maid,
How many may you be?"
"How many? Seven in all," she said,
And wondering looked at me.

"And where are they? I pray you tell."
She answered, "Seven are we;
And two of us at Conway dwell,
And two are gone to sea.

"Two of us in the churchyard lie,
My sister and my brother;
And, in the churchyard cottage, I
Dwell near them with my mother."

"You say that two at Conway dwell,
And two are gone to sea,
Yet ye are seven! I pray you tell,
Sweet maid, how this may be."

Then did the little maid reply,
"Seven boys and girls are we;
Two of us in the churchyard lie,
Beneath the churchyard tree."

"You run about, my little maid,
Your limbs they are alive;
If two are in the churchyard laid,
Then ye are only five."

"Their graves are green, they may be seen,"
The little maid replied,
"Twelve steps or more from my mother's door,
And they are side by side.

"My stockings there I often knit,
My kerchief there I hem;
And there upon the ground I sit,
And sing a song to them.

"And often after sunset, sir,
When it is light and fair,
I take my little porringer,
And eat my supper there.

"The first that died was sister Jane;
In bed she moaning lay,
Till God released her of her pain,
And then she went away.

"So in the churchyard she was laid;
And, when the grass was dry,
Together round her grave we played,
My brother John and I.

"And when the ground was white with snow,
And I could run and slide,
My brother John was forced to go,
And he lies by her side."

"How many are you, then," said I,
"If they two are in heaven?"
Quick was the little maid's reply,
"O master, we are seven."

"But they are dead; those two are dead!
Their spirits are in heaven!"
'Twas throwing words away; for still
The little maid would have her will,
And said, "Nay, we are seven!"

WILLIAM WORDSWORTH

To the Virgins, to Make Much of Time

Gather ye rosebuds while ye may,
　　Old time is still a-flying;
And this same flower that smiles today
　　Tomorrow will be dying.

The glorious lamp of heaven, the sun,
　　The higher he's a-getting,
The sooner will his race be run,
　　And nearer he's to setting.

That age is best which is the first,
　　When youth and blood are warmer;
But being spent, the worse, and worst
　　Times still succeed the former.

Then be not coy, but use your time,
　　And, while ye may, go marry;
For, having lost but once your prime,
　　You may forever tarry.

ROBERT HERRICK

Mother's Nerves

My mother said, "If just once more
I hear you slam that old screen door,
I'll tear out my hair! I'll dive in the stove!"
I gave it a bang and in she dove.

X. J. KENNEDY

He Wishes for the Cloths of Heaven

Had I the heavens' embroidered cloths,
Enwrought with golden and silver light,
The blue and the dim and the dark cloths
Of night and light and the half-light,
I would spread the cloths under your feet:
But I, being poor, have only my dreams;
I have spread my dreams under your feet;
Tread softly because you tread on my dreams.

WILLIAM BUTLER YEATS

The Ship of Rio

There was a ship of Rio
    Sailed out into the blue,
And nine and ninety monkeys
    Were all her jovial crew.
From bo'sun to the cabin boy,
    From quarter to caboose,
There weren't a stitch of calico
    To breech 'em—tight or loose;
From spar to deck, from deck to keel,
    From barnacle to shroud,
There weren't one pair of reach-me-downs
    To all that jabbering crowd.
But wasn't it a gladsome sight,
    When roared the deep-sea gales,
To see them reef her fore and aft,
    A-swinging by their tails!
Oh, wasn't it a gladsome sight,
    When glassy calm did come,
To see them squatting tailor-wise
    Around a keg of rum!
Oh, wasn't it a gladsome sight,
    When in she sailed to land,
To see them all a-scampering skip
    For nuts across the sand!

WALTER DE LA MARE

Western Wind

Westron wind, when will thou blow?
The small rain down can rain.
Christ, that my love were in my arms,
And I in my bed again.

ANONYMOUS

Egrets

Once as I traveled through a quiet evening,
I saw a pool, jet-black and mirror still.
Beyond, the slender paperbarks stood crowding;
each on its own white image looked its fill,
and nothing moved but thirty egrets wading—
thirty egrets in a quiet evening.

Once in a lifetime, lovely past believing,
your lucky eyes may light on such a pool.
As though for many years I had been waiting,
I watched in silence, till my heart was full
of clear dark water, and white trees unmoving,
and, whiter yet, those egrets wading.

JUDITH WRIGHT

The Harlot's House

We caught the tread of dancing feet,
We loitered down the moonlit street,
And stopped beneath the harlot's house.

Inside, above the din and fray,
We heard the loud musicians play
The *Treues Liebes Herz* of Strauss.

Like strange mechanical grotesques,
Making fantastic arabesques,
The shadows raced across the blind.

We watched the ghostly dancers spin
To sound of horn and violin,
Like black leaves wheeling in the wind.

Like wire-pulled automatons,
Slim silhouetted skeletons
Went sidling through the slow quadrille.

They took each other by the hand,
And danced a stately saraband;
Their laughter echoed thin and shrill.

Sometimes a clockwork puppet pressed
A phantom lover to her breast,
Sometimes they seemed to try to sing.

Sometimes a horrible marionette
Came out, and smoked its cigarette
Upon the steps like a live thing.

Then, turning to my love, I said,
"The dead are dancing with the dead,
The dust is whirling with the dust."

But she—she heard the violin,
And left my side, and entered in:
Love passed into the house of lust.

Then suddenly the tune went false,
The dancers wearied of the waltz,
The shadows ceased to wheel and whirl.

And down the long and silent street,
The dawn, with silver-sandaled feet,
Crept like a frightened girl.

OSCAR WILDE

The Night Will Never Stay

The night will never stay,
The night will still go by,
Though with a million stars
You pin it to the sky;
Though you bind it with the blowing wind
And buckle it with the moon,
The night will slip away
Like sorrow or a tune.

ELEANOR FARJEON

Tree at My Window

Tree at my window, window tree,
My sash is lowered when night comes on;
But let there never be curtain drawn
Between you and me.

Vague dream-head lifted out of the ground,
And thing next most diffuse to cloud,
Not all your light tongues talking aloud
Could be profound.

But, tree, I have seen you taken and tossed,
And if you have seen me when I slept,
You have seen me when I was taken and swept
And all but lost.

That day she put our heads together,
Fate had her imagination about her,
Your head so much concerned with outer,
Mine with inner, weather.

ROBERT FROST

Cavalry Crossing a Ford

A line in long array where they wind betwixt green islands,
They take a serpentine course, their arms flash in the sun—hark
    to the musical clank,
Behold the silvery river, in it the splashing horses loitering stop
    to drink,
Behold the brown-faced men, each group, each person a picture,
    the negligent rest on the saddles,
Some emerge on the opposite bank, others are just entering the
    ford—while,
Scarlet and blue and snowy white,
The guidon flags flutter gaily in the wind.

WALT WHITMAN

Contingency

Water from the sprinkler
collects
in street-edge gravel and
makes rocky pools: birds
materialize—puff, bathe
and drink: a green-black

grackle lopes, listing,
across the hot street, pecks
a starling, and drinks: a

robin rears misty with
exultation: twittering comes
in bunches of starts and
flights: shadows pour
across cement and lawn: a
turn of the faucet
dries every motion up.

                              A. R. AMMONS

Dust of Snow

The way a crow
Shook down on me
The dust of snow
From a hemlock tree

Has given my heart
A change of mood
And saved some part
Of a day I had rued.

ROBERT FROST

The Snow Man

One must have a mind of winter
To regard the frost and the boughs
Of the pine-trees crusted with snow;

And have been cold a long time
To behold the junipers shagged with ice,
The spruces rough in the distant glitter

Of the January sun; and not to think
Of any misery in the sound of the wind,
In the sound of a few leaves,

Which is the sound of the land
Full of the same wind
That is blowing in the same bare place

For the listener, who listens in the snow,
And, nothing himself, beholds
Nothing that is not there and the nothing that is.

WALLACE STEVENS

Boy at the Window

Seeing the snowman standing all alone
In dusk and cold is more than he can bear.
The small boy weeps to hear the wind prepare
A night of gnashings and enormous moan.
His tearful sight can hardly reach to where
The pale-faced figure with bitumen eyes
Returns him such a god-forsaken stare
As outcast Adam gave to Paradise.

The man of snow is, nonetheless, content,
Having no wish to go inside and die.
Still, he is moved to see the youngster cry.
Though frozen water is his element,
He melts enough to drop from one soft eye
A trickle of the purest rain, a tear
For the child at the bright pane surrounded by
Such warmth, such light, such love, and so much fear.

RICHARD WILBUR

This Is Just to Say

I have eaten
the plums
that were in
the icebox

and which
you were probably
saving
for breakfast

Forgive me
they were delicious
so sweet
and so cold

WILLIAM CARLOS WILLIAMS

Harlem

What happens to a dream deferred?

Does it dry up
like a raisin in the sun?
Or fester like a sore—
And then run?
Does it stink like rotten meat?
Or crust and sugar over—
like a syrupy sweet?

Maybe it just sags
like a heavy load.

Or does it explode?

LANGSTON HUGHES

When I was one-and-twenty
  I heard a wise man say,
"Give crowns and pounds and guineas,
  But not your heart, away;
Give pearls away and rubies,
  But keep your fancy free."
But I was one-and-twenty—
  No use to talk to me.

When I was one-and-twenty
  I heard him say again,
"The heart out of the bosom
  Was never given in vain;
'Tis paid with sighs a plenty
  And sold for endless rue."
And I am two-and-twenty,
  And oh, 'tis true, 'tis true.

A. E. HOUSMAN

My Papa's Waltz

The whiskey on your breath
Could make a small boy dizzy;
But I hung on like death:
Such waltzing was not easy.

We romped until the pans
Slid from the kitchen shelf;
My mother's countenance
Could not unfrown itself.

The hand that held my wrist
Was battered on one knuckle;
At every step you missed
My right ear scraped a buckle.

You beat time on my head
With a palm caked hard by dirt,
Then waltzed me off to bed
Still clinging to your shirt.

THEODORE ROETHKE

Soliloquy of a Tortoise

on Revisiting

the Lettuce Beds

After an Interval of One Hour

While Supposed

to Be

Sleeping

in a Clump

of Blue Hollyhocks

One cannot have enough
of this delicious stuff!

E.V. RIEU

To Daffodils

Fair daffodils, we weep to see
  You haste away so soon:
As yet the early rising sun
  Has not attained his noon.
    Stay, stay,
  Until the hasting day
    Has run
  But to the Evensong;
And, having prayed together, we
  Will go with you along.

We have short time to stay, as you,
  We have as short a spring;
As quick a growth to meet decay,
  As you, or any thing.
    We die,
  As your hours do, and dry
    Away,
  Like to the summer's rain;
Or as the pearls of morning's dew
  Ne'er to be found again.

                    ROBERT HERRICK

The Outlandish Knight

An outlandish knight came from the North
  A-wooing with buckler and blade;
And he promised to take her into the North,
  And there he would marry the maid.

"Come fetch me some of your father's gold
  And some of your mother's fee;
And two of the best nags out of the stable,
  Where they stand thirty and three."

She fetched him some of her father's gold
  And some of her mother's fee;
And two of the best nags out of the stable,
  Where they stood thirty and three.

She mounted her on her milk-white steed,
  He on the dapple gray;
They rode till they came unto the sea-side,
  Three hours before it was day.

"Light off, light off thy milk-white steed,
  And deliver it unto me;
Six pretty maids have I drowned here,
  And thou the seventh shall be.

"Pull off, pull off thy silken gown,
  And deliver it unto me,
Methinks it looks too rich and too gay
  To rot in the salt, salt sea.

"Pull off, pull off thy silken stays,
  And deliver them unto me!
Methinks they are too fine and gay
  To rot in the salt, salt sea.

"Pull off, pull off thy Holland smock,
   And deliver it unto me;
Methinks it looks too rich and gay
   To rot in the salt, salt sea."

"If I must pull off my Holland smock,
   Pray turn thy back unto me,
For it is not fitting that such a ruffian
   A woman unclad should see."

He turned his back towards her,
   And looked to the leaf of the tree;
She caught him round the middle so small,
   And tumbled him into the sea.

He dropped high, and he dropped low,
   Until he came to the tide—
"Catch hold of my hand, my pretty maiden,
   And I will make you my bride."

"Lie there, lie there, you false-hearted man,
   Lie there instead of me;
Six pretty maidens have you drowned here,
   And the seventh has drowned thee."

She mounted on her milk-white steed,
   And led the dapple gray,
She rode till she came to her father's hall,
   Three hours before it was day.

ANONYMOUS

The 1st

What I remember about that day
is boxes stacked across the walk
and couch springs curling through the air
and drawers and tables balanced on the curb
and us, hollering,
leaping up and around
happy to have a playground;

nothing about the emptied rooms
nothing about the emptied family

LUCILLE CLIFTON

Concord Hymn

SUNG AT THE COMPLETION OF THE BATTLE
MONUMENT, JULY 4, 1837

By the rude bridge that arched the flood,
  Their flag to April's breeze unfurled,
Here once the embattled farmers stood
  And fired the shot heard round the world.

The foe long since in silence slept;
  Alike the conqueror silent sleeps;
And Time the ruined bridge has swept
  Down the dark stream which seaward creeps.

On this green bank, by this soft stream,
  We set to-day a votive stone;
That memory may their deed redeem,
  When, like our sires, our sons are gone.

Spirit, that made those heroes dare
  To die, and leave their children free.
Bid Time and Nature gently spare
  The shaft we raise to them and thee.

RALPH WALDO EMERSON

Believe Me, If All Those Endearing Young Charms

Believe me, if all those endearing young charms,
   Which I gaze on so fondly today,
Were to change by tomorrow, and fleet in my arms,
   Like fairy-gifts fading away,
Thou wouldst still be adored, as this moment thou art,
   Let thy loveliness fade as it will,
And around the dear ruin each wish of my heart
   Would entwine itself verdantly still.

It is not while beauty and youth are thine own,
   And thy cheeks unprofaned by a tear
That the fervor and faith of a soul can be known,
   To which time will but make thee more dear;
No, the heart that has truly loved never forgets,
   But as truly loves on to the close,
As the sunflower turns on her god, when he sets,
   The same look which she turned when he rose.

THOMAS MOORE

What Tomas Said in a Pub

I saw God!   Do you doubt it?
Do you dare to doubt it?
I saw the Almighty Man!   His hand
Was resting on a mountain!   And
He looked upon the World, and all about it:
I saw Him plainer than you see me now
—You mustn't doubt it!

He was not satisfied!
His look was all dissatisfied!
His beard swung on a wind, far out of sight
Behind the world's curve!   And there was light
Most fearful from His forehead!   And He sighed—
—That star went always wrong, and from the start
I was dissatisfied!—

He lifted up His hand!
I say He heaved a dreadful hand
Over the spinning earth!   Then I said, —Stay,
You must not strike it, God!   I'm in the way!
And I will never move from where I stand!—
He said, —Dear child, I feared that you were dead,—
. . . And stayed His hand!

JAMES STEPHENS

Rain

The rain is raining all around,
  It falls on field and tree,
It rains on the umbrellas here,
  And on the ships at sea.

ROBERT LOUIS STEVENSON

My Brother Bert

Pets are the hobby of my brother Bert.
He used to go to school with a mouse in his shirt.

His hobby it grew, as some hobbies will,
And grew and GREW and GREW until—

Oh don't breathe a word, pretend you haven't heard.
A simply appalling thing has occurred—

The very thought makes me iller and iller:
Bert's brought home a gigantic gorilla!

If you think that's really not such a scare,
What if it quarrels with his grizzly bear?

You still think you could keep your head?
What if the lion from under the bed

And the four ostriches that deposit
Their football eggs in his bedroom closet

And the aardvark out of his bottom drawer
All danced out and joined in the roar?

What if the pangolins were to caper
Out of their nests behind the wallpaper?

With the fifty sorts of bats
That hang on his hatstand like old hats,

And out of a shoebox the excitable platypus
Along with the ocelot or jungle-cattypus?

The wombat, the dingo, the gecko, the grampus—
How they would shake the house with their rumpus!

Not to forget the bandicoot
Who would certainly peer from his battered old boot.

Why it could be a dreadful day,
And what, oh what, would the neighbors say!

TED HUGHES

133

The Foggy Dew

When I was a bachelor early and young,
   I followed the weaving trade,
And all the harm ever I done,
   Was courting a servant maid.
I courted her the summer season,
   And part of the winter too,
And many a night I rolled her in my arms,
   All over the foggy dew.

One night as I lay on my bed,
   As I laid fast asleep,
There came a pretty fair maid,
   And most bitterly did weep.
She wept she mourned she tore her hair,
   Crying, alas what shall I do,
This night I'm resolved to come to bed with you
   For fear of the foggy dew.

It was in the first part of the night,
   We both did sport and play,
And in the latter part of the night,
   She slept in my arms till day.
When broad day-light did appear,
   She cried I am undone,
Hold your tongue you foolish girl,
   The foggy dew is gone.

Suppose that we should have a child,
   It would cause us to smile,
Suppose that we should have another
   It would make us laugh awhile.
Suppose that we should have another,
   And another one too,
Would make you leave off your foolish tricks
   And think no more of the foggy dew.

I love this young girl dearly,
   I loved her as my life,
Took this girl and married her,
   And made her my lawful wife.
Never told her of her faults,
   Nor never intend to do,
But every time she winks or smiles,
   She thinks of the foggy dew.

ANONYMOUS

Answer to a Child's Question

Do you ask what the birds say? The sparrow, the dove,
The linnet and thrush say, "I love and I love!"
In the winter they're silent—the wind is so strong;
What it says, I don't know, but it sings a loud song.
But green leaves, and blossoms, and sunny warm weather,
And singing, and loving—all come back together.
But the lark is so brimful of gladness and love,
The green fields below him, the blue sky above,
That he sings, and he sings; and for ever sings he—
"I love my Love, and my Love loves me!"

SAMUEL TAYLOR COLERIDGE

Too Many Daves

Did I ever tell you that Mrs. McCave
Had twenty-three sons and she named them all Dave?
Well, she did. And that wasn't a smart thing to do.
You see, when she wants one and calls out, "Yoo-Hoo!
Come into the house, Dave!" she doesn't get *one*.
All twenty-three Daves of hers come on the run!
This makes things quite difficult at the McCaves'
As you can imagine, with so many Daves.
And often she wishes that, when they were born,
She had named one of them Bodkin Van Horn
And one of them Hoos-Foos. And one of them Snimm.
And one of them Hot-Shot. And one Sunny Jim.
And one of them Shadrack. And one of them Blinkey.
And one of them Stuffy. And one of them Stinkey.
Another one Putt-Putt. Another one Moon Face.
Another one Marvin O'Gravel Balloon Face.
And one of them Ziggy. And one Soggy Muff.
One Buffalo Bill. And one Biffalo Buff.
And one of them Sneepy. And one Weepy Weed.
And one Paris Garters. And one Harris Tweed.
And one of them Sir Michael Carmichael Zutt
And one of them Oliver Boliver Butt
And one of them Zanzibar Buck-Buck McFate . . .
But she didn't do it. And now it's too late.

DR. SEUSS

The Owl

When cats run home and light is come,
  And dew is cold upon the ground,
And the far-off stream is dumb,
  And the whirring sail goes round,
  And the whirring sail goes round:
    Alone and warming his five wits,
    The white owl in the belfry sits.

When merry milkmaids click the latch,
  And rarely smells the new-mown hay,
And the cock hath sung beneath the thatch
  Twice or thrice his roundelay,
  Twice or thrice his roundelay:
    Alone and warming his five wits,
    The white owl in the belfry sits.

ALFRED, LORD TENNYSON

The Water-Ousel

Where on the wrinkled stream the willows lean,
And fling a very ecstasy of green
Down the dim crystal; and the chestnut tree
Admires her large-leaved shadow, swift and free,
A water-ousel came, with such a flight
As archangels might envy. Soft and bright
Upon a water-kissing bough she lit,
And washed and preened her silver breast, though it
Was dazzling fair before. Then twittering
She sang, and made obeisance to the Spring.
And in the wavering amber at her feet
Her silent shadow, with obedience meet,
Made her quick, imitative curtsies, too.
Maybe she dreamed a nest, so safe and dear,
Where the keen spray leaps whitely to the weir;
And smooth, warm eggs that hold a mystery;
And stirrings of life and twitterings, that she
Is passionately glad of; and a breast
As silver-white as hers, which without rest
Or languor, borne by spread wings swift and strong,
Shall fly upon her service all day long.
She hears a presage in the ancient thunder
Of the silken fall, and her small soul in wonder
Makes preparation as she deems most right,
Repurifying what before was white
Against the day when, like a beautiful dream,
Two little ousels shall fly with her down stream,
And even the poor, dumb shadow-bird shall flit
With two small shadows following after it.

MARY WEBB

139

Recuerdo

We were very tired, we were very merry—
We had gone back and forth all night on the ferry.
It was bare and bright, and smelled like a stable—
But we looked into a fire, we leaned across a table,
We lay on the hill-top underneath the moon;
And the whistles kept blowing, and the dawn came soon.

We were very tired, we were very merry—
We had gone back and forth all night on the ferry;
And you ate an apple, and I ate a pear,
From a dozen of each we had bought somewhere;
And the sky went wan, and the wind came cold,
And the sun rose dripping, a bucketful of gold.

We were very tired, we were very merry—
We had gone back and forth all night on the ferry.
We hailed, "Good morrow, mother!" to a shawl-covered head,
And bought a morning paper, which neither of us read;
And she wept, "God bless you!" for the apples and the pears,
And we gave her all our money but our subway fares.

EDNA ST. VINCENT MILLAY

Cats

Cats sleep
Anywhere,
Any table,
Any chair,
Top of piano,
Window-ledge,
In the middle,
On the edge,
Open drawer,
Empty shoe,
Anybody's
Lap will do,
Fitted in a
Cardboard box,
In the cupboard
With your frocks—
Anywhere!
They don't care!
Cats sleep
Anywhere.

ELEANOR FARJEON

Elsa Wertman

I was a peasant girl from Germany,
Blue-eyed, rosy, happy and strong.
And the first place I worked was at Thomas Greene's.
On a summer's day when she was away
He stole into the kitchen and took me
Right in his arms and kissed me on my throat,
I turning my head. Then neither of us
Seemed to know what happened.
And I cried for what would become of me.
And cried and cried as my secret began to show.
One day Mrs. Greene said she understood,
And would make no trouble for me,
And, being childless, would adopt it.
(He had given her a farm to be still.)
So she hid in the house and sent out rumors,
As if it were going to happen to her.
And all went well and the child was born—They were so kind
          to me.
Later I married Gus Wertman, and years passed.
But—at political rallies when sitters-by thought I was crying
At the eloquence of Hamilton Greene—
That was not it.
No!   I wanted to say:
That's my son!   That's my son!

Hamilton Greene

I was the only child of Frances Harris of Virginia
And Thomas Greene of Kentucky,
Of valiant and honorable blood both.
To them I owe all that I became,
Judge, member of Congress, leader in the State.
From my mother I inherited

Vivacity, fancy, language;
From my father will, judgment, logic.
All honor to them
For what service I was to the people!

EDGAR LEE MASTERS

The Pear Tree

In this squalid, dirty dooryard
  Where the chickens squawk and run,
White, incredible, the pear tree
  Stands apart, and takes the sun;

Mindful of the eyes upon it,
  Vain of its new holiness,—
Like the waste-man's little daughter
  In her First Communion dress.

EDNA ST. VINCENT MILLAY

Loveliest of trees, the cherry now
Is hung with bloom along the bough,
And stands about the woodland ride
Wearing white for Eastertide.

Now, of my threescore years and ten,
Twenty will not come again,
And take from seventy springs a score,
It only leaves me fifty more.

And since to look at things in bloom
Fifty springs are little room,
About the woodlands I will go
To see the cherry hung with snow.

A. E. HOUSMAN

Danny Deever

"What are the bugles blowin' for?" said Files-on-Parade.
"To turn you out, to turn you out," the Color-Sergeant said.
"What makes you look so white, so white?" said
    Files-on-Parade.
"I'm dreadin' what I've got to watch," the Color-Sergeant said.
    For they're hangin' Danny Deever, you can hear the Dead
      March play.
    The Regiment's in 'ollow square—they're hangin' him
      today;
    They've taken of his buttons off an' cut his stripes away,
    An' they're hangin' Danny Deever in the mornin'.

"What makes the rear-rank breathe so 'ard?" said
    Files-on-Parade.
"It's bitter cold, it's bitter cold," the Color-Sergeant said.
"What makes that front-rank man fall down?" said
    Files-on-Parade.
"A touch o'sun, a touch o'sun," the Color-Sergeant said.
    They are hangin' Danny Deever, they are marchin' of 'im
      round.
    They 'ave 'alted Danny Deever by 'is coffin on the ground;
    And 'e'll swing in 'arf a minute for a sneakin' shootin'
      hound—
    O they're hangin' Danny Deever in the mornin'!

" 'Is cot was right-'and cot to mine," said Files-on-Parade.
" 'E's sleepin' out an' far tonight," the Color-Sergeant said.
"I've drunk 'is beer a score o' times," said Files-on-Parade.
" 'E's drinkin' bitter beer alone," the Color-Sergeant said.
    They are hangin' Danny Deever, you must mark 'im to 'is
      place,
    For 'e shot a comrade sleepin'—you must look 'im in the
      face;
    Nine 'undred of 'is county an' the Regiment's disgrace,
    While they're hangin' Danny Deever in the mornin'.

"What's that so black agin the sun?" said Files-on-Parade.
"It's Danny fightin' 'ard for life," the Color-Sergeant said.
"What's that that whimpers over'ead?" said Files-on-Parade.
"It's Danny's soul that's passin' now," the Color-Sergeant said.
  For they're done with Danny Deever, you can 'ear the
    quickstep play,
  The Regiment's in column, an' they're marchin' us away;
  Ho! the young recruits are shakin', an' they'll want their
    beer today,
  After hangin' Danny Deever in the mornin'!

RUDYARD KIPLING

The Lake Isle of Innisfree

I will arise and go now, and go to Innisfree,
And a small cabin build there, of clay and wattles made:
Nine bean-rows will I have there, a hive for the honey bee,
And live alone in the bee-loud glade.

And I shall have some peace there, for peace comes dropping
    slow,
Dropping from the veils of the morning to where the cricket
    sings;
There midnight's all a glimmer, and noon a purple glow,
And evening full of the linnet's wings.

I will arise and go now, for always night and day
I hear lake water lapping with low sounds by the shore;
While I stand on the roadway, or on the pavements gray,
I hear it in the deep heart's core.

WILLIAM BUTLER YEATS

The River-Merchant's Wife: A Letter

While my hair was still cut straight across my forehead
I played about the front gate, pulling flowers.
You came by on bamboo stilts, playing horse,
You walked about my seat, playing with blue plums.
And we went on living in the village of Chokan:
Two small people, without dislike or suspicion.

At fourteen I married My Lord you.
I never laughed, being bashful.
Lowering my head, I looked at the wall.
Called to, a thousand times, I never looked back.

At fifteen I stopped scowling,
I desired my dust to be mingled with yours
For ever and for ever and for ever.
Why should I climb the look out?

At sixteen you departed,
You went into far Ku-to-yen, by the river of swirling eddies,
And you have been gone five months.
The monkeys make sorrowful noise overhead.

You dragged your feet when you went out.
By the gate now, the moss is grown, the different mosses,
Too deep to clear them away!
The leaves fall early this autumn, in wind.
The paired butterflies are already yellow with August
Over the grass in the West garden;
They hurt me. I grow older.
If you are coming down through the narrows of the river Kiang,
Please let me know beforehand,
And I will come out to meet you
                    As far as Cho-fu-Sa.

EZRA POUND

Richard Cory

Whenever Richard Cory went down town,
    We people on the pavement looked at him:
He was a gentleman from sole to crown,
    Clean favored, and imperially slim.

And he was always quietly arrayed,
    And he was always human when he talked;
But still he fluttered pulses when he said,
    "Good-morning," and he glittered when he walked.

And he was rich—yes, richer than a king,
    And admirably schooled in every grace:
In fine, we thought that he was everything
    To make us wish that we were in his place.

So on we worked, and waited for the light,
    And went without the meat, and cursed the bread;
And Richard Cory, one calm summer night,
    Went home and put a bullet through his head.

EDWIN ARLINGTON ROBINSON

Thirteen Ways
of Looking at
a Blackbird

I

Among twenty snowy mountains,
The only moving thing
Was the eye of the blackbird.

II

I was of three minds,
Like a tree
In which there are three blackbirds.

III

The blackbird whirled in the autumn winds.
It was a small part of the pantomime.

IV

A man and a woman
Are one.
A man and a woman and a blackbird
Are one.

V

I do not know which to prefer,
The beauty of inflections
Or the beauty of innuendoes,
The blackbird whistling
Or just after.

VI

Icicles filled the long window
With barbaric glass.
The shadow of the blackbird
Crossed it, to and fro.

The mood
Traced in the shadow
An indecipherable cause.

VII

O thin men of Haddam,
Why do you imagine golden birds?
Do you not see how the blackbird
Walks around the feet
Of the women about you?

VIII

I know noble accents
And lucid, inescapable rhythms;
But I know, too,
That the blackbird is involved
In what I know.

IX

When the blackbird flew out of sight,
It marked the edge
Of one of many circles.

X

At the sight of blackbirds
Flying in a green light,
Even the bawds of euphony
Would cry out sharply.

XI

He rode over Connecticut
In a glass coach.
Once, a fear pierced him,
In that he mistook
The shadow of his equipage
For blackbirds.

XII

The river is moving.
The blackbird must be flying.

XIII

It was evening all afternoon.
It was snowing
And it was going to snow.
The blackbird sat
In the cedar-limbs.

WALLACE STEVENS

O What Is That Sound

O what is that sound which so thrills the ear
   Down in the valley drumming, drumming?
Only the scarlet soldiers, dear,
   The soldiers coming.

O what is that light I see flashing so clear
   Over the distance brightly, brightly?
Only the sun on their weapons, dear,
   As they step lightly.

O what are they doing with all that gear,
   What are they doing this morning, this morning?
Only their usual maneuvers, dear,
   Or perhaps a warning.

O why have they left the road down there,
   Why are they suddenly wheeling, wheeling?
Perhaps a change in their orders, dear.
   Why are you kneeling?

O haven't they stopped for the doctor's care,
   Haven't they reined their horses, their horses?
Why, they are none of them wounded, dear,
   None of these forces.

O is it the parson they want, with white hair,
   Is it the parson, is it, is it?
No, they are passing his gateway, dear,
   Without a visit.

O it must be the farmer who lives so near.
   It must be the farmer so cunning, so cunning?
They have passed the farmyard already, dear,
   And now they are running.

O where are you going? Stay with me here!
   Were the vows you swore deceiving, deceiving?
No, I promised to love you, dear,
   But I must be leaving.

O it's broken the lock and splintered the door,
  O it's the gate where they're turning, turning;
Their boots are heavy on the floor
  And their eyes are burning.

W. H. AUDEN

Water Ouzel

FOR DORA WILLSON

Follow back from the gull's bright arc and the osprey's plunge,
Past the silent heron, erect in the tidal marsh,
Up the mighty river, rolling in mud. Branch off
At the sign of the kingfisher poised on a twisted snag.
Not deceived when the surface grows calm, keep on,
Past the placidity of ducks, the delusive pastoral dreams
Drawn down by the effortless swallows that drink on the wing.
With the wheat fields behind you, do not neglect to choose
At every juncture the clearest and coldest path.
Push through the reeds where the redwing sways,
Climb through the warnings of hidden jays,
Climb, climb the jostling, narrowing stream
Through aspen sunlight into the evergreen darkness
Where chattering crossbills scatter the shreds of cones.
Here at last at the brink of the furthest fall,
With the water dissolving to mist as it shatters the pool below,
Pause beneath timber-line springs and the melting snow.
Here, where the shadows are deep in the crystal air,
So near a myriad beginnings, after so long a journey,
Expecting at least a golden cockatoo
Or a screaming eagle with wings of flame,
Stifle your disappointment, observe
The burgher of all this beauty, the drab
Citizen of the headwaters; struggle to love
The ridiculous ouzel, perched on his slippery stone
Like an awkward, overblown catbird deprived of its tail.

Not for him the limitless soaring above the storm,
Or the surface-skimming, or swimming, or plunging in.
He walks. In the midst of the turbulence, bathed in spray,
From a rock without foothold into the lunging current
He descends a deliberate step at a time till, submerged,
He has walked from sight and hope. The stream

Drives on, dashes, splashes, drops over the edge,
Too swift for ice in midwinter, too cold
For life in midsummer, depositing any debris,
Leaf, twig or carcass, along the way,
Wedging them in behind rocks to rot,
Such as these not reaching the ocean.

Yet, lo, the lost one emerges unharmed,
Hardly wet as he walks from the water.
Undisturbed by beauty or terror, pursuing
His own few needs with a nerveless will,
Nonchalant in the torrent, he bobs and nods
As though to acknowledge implicit applause.
This ceaseless tic, a trick of the muscles shared
With the solitary sandpiper, burlesqued
By the teeter-bob and the phoebe's tail,
Is not related to approbation. The dipper,
Denied the adventure of uncharted flight
Over vast waters to an unknown homeland, denied
Bodily beauty, slightly absurd and eccentric,
Will never attain acclaim as a popular hero.
No prize committee selects the clown
Whose only dangers are daily and domestic.

Yet he persists, and does not consider it persisting.
On a starless, sub-zero, northern night,
When all else has taken flight into sleep or the south,
He, on the edge of the stream, has been heard to repeat
The rippling notes of his song, which are clear and sweet.

WILLIAM H. MATCHETT

Proud Songsters

The thrushes sing as the sun is going,
  And the finches whistle in ones and pairs,
And as it gets dark loud nightingales
    In bushes
Pipe, as they can when April wears,
  As if all Time were theirs.

These are brand new birds of twelve-months' growing,
Which a year ago, or less than twain,
No finches were, nor nightingales,
    Nor thrushes,
But only particles of grain,
  And earth, and air, and rain.

THOMAS HARDY

To the Snake

Green Snake, when I hung you round my neck
and stroked your cold, pulsing throat
    as you hissed to me, glinting
arrowy gold scales, and I felt
    the weight of you on my shoulders,
and the whispering silver of your dryness
    sounded close at my ears—

Green Snake—I swore to my companions that certainly
    you were harmless! But truly
I had no certainty, and no hope, only desiring
    to hold you, for that joy,
                which left
a long wake of pleasure, as the leaves moved
and you faded into the pattern
of grass and shadows, and I returned
smiling and haunted, to a dark morning.

DENISE LEVERTOV

Father and Mother

My father's name is Frankenstein,
He comes from the Barbados.
He fashioned me from package twine
And instant mashed potatoes.

My mother's name is Draculeen,
She lets a big bat bite her,
And folks who sleep here overnight
Wake up a few quarts lighter.

X. J. KENNEDY

Winter was a white page

soon to be ripped
  from the calendar
    says the rippling script
          of Canada geese
            in a language
              their quills
                bring creaking
                  from valleys
                  and bristling hills
                    where it entered
                      the redman's deep
                        ancestral sleep
                        a message
                        that stirred
                      the bear in its bed
                      the grasses
                    under snow
                a message heard
                and read
              at an open
              window
            by one
          whose
        pen
        passes
      the
      word

JON STALLWORTHY

My Last Duchess

FERRARA

That's my last duchess painted on the wall,
Looking as if she were alive. I call
That piece a wonder, now: Frà Pandolf's hands
Worked busily a day, and there she stands.
Will't please you sit and look at her? I said
"Frà Pandolf" by design, for never read
Strangers like you that pictured countenance,
The depth and passion of its earnest glance,
But to myself they turned (since none puts by
The curtain I have drawn for you, but I)
And seemed as they would ask me, if they durst,
How such a glance came there; so, not the first
Are you to turn and ask thus. Sir, 'twas not
Her husband's presence only, called that spot
Of joy into the Duchess' cheek: perhaps
Frà Pandolf chanced to say "Her mantle laps
"Over my lady's wrist too much," or "Paint
"Must never hope to reproduce the faint
"Half-flush that dies along her throat": such stuff
Was courtesy, she thought, and cause enough
For calling up that spot of joy. She had
A heart—how shall I say?—too soon made glad,
Too easily impressed; she liked whate'er
She looked on, and her looks went everywhere.
Sir, 'twas all one! My favor at her breast,
The dropping of the daylight in the West,
The bough of cherries some officious fool
Broke in the orchard for her, the white mule
She rode with round the terrace—all and each
Would draw from her alike the approving speech,
Or blush, at least. She thanked men—good! but thanked
Somehow—I know not how—as if she ranked
My gift of a nine-hundred-years-old name

With anybody's gift. Who'd stoop to blame
This sort of trifling? Even had you skill
In speech—which I have not—to make your will
Quite clear to such an one, and say, "Just this
"Or that in you disgusts me; here you miss,
"Or there exceed the mark"—and if she let
Herself be lessoned so, nor plainly set
Her wits to yours, forsooth, and made excuse,
—E'en then would be some stooping; and I choose
Never to stoop. Oh sir, she smiled, no doubt,
Whene'er I passed her; but who passed without
Much the same smile? This grew; I gave commands;
Then all smiles stopped together. There she stands
As if alive. Will 't please you rise? We'll meet
The company below, then. I repeat,
The Count your master's known munificence
Is ample warrant that no just pretense
Of mine for dowry will be disallowed;
Though his fair daughter's self, as I avowed
At starting, is my object. Nay, we'll go
Together down, sir. Notice Neptune, though,
Taming a sea-horse, thought a rarity,
Which Claus of Innsbruck cast in bronze for me!

ROBERT BROWNING

Sweet and Low

Sweet and low, sweet and low,
   Wind of the western sea!
Low, low, breathe and blow,
   Wind of the western sea!
Over the rolling waters go,
Come from the dying moon, and blow,
   Blow him again to me;
While my little one, while my pretty one, sleeps.

Sleep and rest, sleep and rest,
   Father will come to thee soon;
Rest, rest, on mother's breast,
   Father will come to thee soon;
Father will come to his babe in the nest,
Silver sails all out of the west
   Under the silver moon;
Sleep, my little one, sleep, my pretty one, sleep.

ALFRED, LORD TENNYSON

Four ducks on a pond,
A grass-bank beyond,
A blue sky of spring,
White clouds on the wing:
What a little thing
To remember for years—
To remember with tears!

WILLIAM ALLINGHAM

System

Every night my prayers I say,
And get my dinner every day;
And every day that I've been good,
I get an orange after food.

The child that is not clean and neat,
With lots of toys and things to eat,
He is a naughty child, I'm sure—
Or else his dear papa is poor.

ROBERT LOUIS STEVENSON

The Paint Box

"Cobalt and umber and ultramarine,
Ivory black and emerald green—
What shall I paint to give pleasure to you?"
"Paint for me somebody utterly new."

"I have painted you tigers in crimson and white."
"The colors were good and you painted aright."
"I have painted the cook and a camel in blue
And a panther in purple." "You painted them true.

"Now mix me a color that nobody knows,
And paint me a country where nobody goes.
And put in it people a little like you,
Watching a unicorn drinking the dew."

E. V. RIEU

A Frosty Night

"Alice, dear, what ails you,
   Dazed and lost and shaken?
Has the chill night numbed you?
   Is it fright you have taken?"

"Mother, I am very well,
   I was never better.
Mother, do not hold me so,
   Let me write my letter."

"Sweet, my dear, what ails you?"
   "No, but I am well.
The night was cold and frosty—
   There's no more to tell."

"Ay, the night was frosty,
   Coldly gaped the moon,
Yet the birds seemed twittering
   Through green boughs of June.

"Soft and thick the snow lay,
   Stars danced in the sky—
Not all the lambs of May-day
   Skip so bold and high.

"Your feet were dancing, Alice,
   Seemed to dance on air,
You looked a ghost or angel
   In the star-light there.

"Your eyes were frosted star-light;
   Your heart, fire and snow.
Who was it said, 'I love you'?"
   "Mother, let me go!"

ROBERT GRAVES

The Fish

I caught a tremendous fish
and held him beside the boat
half out of water, with my hook
fast in a corner of his mouth.
He didn't fight.
He hadn't fought at all.
He hung a grunting weight,
battered and venerable
and homely. Here and there
his brown skin hung in strips
like ancient wallpaper,
and its pattern of darker brown
was like wallpaper:
shapes like full-blown roses
stained and lost through age.
He was speckled with barnacles,
fine rosettes of lime,
and infested
with tiny white sea-lice,
and underneath two or three
rags of green weed hung down.
While his gills were breathing in
the terrible oxygen
—the frightening gills,
fresh and crisp with blood,
that can cut so badly—
I thought of the coarse white flesh
packed in like feathers,
the big bones and the little bones,
the dramatic reds and blacks
of his shiny entrails,
and the pink swim-bladder
like a big peony.
I looked into his eyes

which were far larger than mine
but shallower, and yellowed,
the irises backed and packed
with tarnished tinfoil
seen through the lenses
of old scratched isinglass.
They shifted a little, but not
to return my stare.
—It was more like the tipping
of an object toward the light.
I admired his sullen face,
the mechanism of his jaw,
and then I saw
that from his lower lip
—if you could call it a lip—
grim, wet, and weaponlike,
hung five old pieces of fish-line,
or four and a wire leader
with the swivel still attached,
with all their five big hooks
grown firmly in his mouth.
A green line, frayed at the end
where he broke it, two heavier lines,
and a fine black thread
still crimped from the strain and snap
when it broke and he got away.
Like medals with their ribbons
frayed and wavering,
a five-haired beard of wisdom
trailing from his aching jaw.
I stared and stared
and victory filled up
the little rented boat,
from the pool of bilge
where oil had spread a rainbow
around the rusted engine
to the bailer rusted orange,

the sun-cracked thwarts,
the oarlocks on their strings,
the gunnels—until everything
was rainbow, rainbow, rainbow!
And I let the fish go.

ELIZABETH BISHOP

A Song in the Front Yard

I've stayed in the front yard all my life.
I want a peek at the back
Where it's rough and untended and hungry weed grows.
A girl gets sick of a rose.

I want to go in the back yard now
And maybe down the alley,
To where the charity children play.
I want a good time today.

They do some wonderful things.
They have some wonderful fun.
My mother sneers, but I say it's fine
How they don't have to go in at quarter to nine.
My mother, she tells me that Johnnie Mae
Will grow up to be a bad woman.
That George'll be taken to Jail soon or late
(On account of last winter he sold our back gate).

But I say it's fine. Honest, I do.
And I'd like to be a bad woman, too,
And wear the brave stockings of night-black lace
And strut down the streets with paint on my face.

GWENDOLYN BROOKS

What Is Pink?

What is pink? a rose is pink
By the fountain's brink.
What is red? a poppy's red
In its barley bed.
What is blue? the sky is blue
Where the clouds float thro'
What is white? a swan is white
Sailing in the light.
What is yellow? pears are yellow,
Rich and ripe and mellow.
What is green? the grass is green,
With small flowers between.
What is violet? clouds are violet
In the summer twilight.
What is orange? why, an orange,
Just an orange!

CHRISTINA ROSSETTI

Macavity: the Mystery Cat

Macavity's a Mystery Cat: he's called the Hidden Paw—
For he's the master criminal who can defy the Law.
He's the bafflement of Scotland Yard, the Flying Squad's
    despair:
For when they reach the scene of crime—*Macavity's not there!*

Macavity, Macavity, there's no one like Macavity,
He's broken every human law, he breaks the law of gravity.
His powers of levitation would make a fakir stare,
And when you reach the scene of crime—*Macavity's not there!*
You may seek him in the basement, you may look up in the
    air—
But I tell you once and once again, *Macavity's not there!*

Macavity's a ginger cat, he's very tall and thin;
You would know him if you saw him, for his eyes are sunken
    in.
His brow is deeply lined with thought, his head is highly
    domed;
His coat is dusty from neglect, his whiskers are uncombed.
He sways his head from side to side, with movements like a
    snake;
And when you think he's half asleep, he's always wide awake.

Macavity, Macavity, there's no one like Macavity,
For he's a fiend in feline shape, a monster of depravity.
You may meet him in a by-street, you may see him in the
    square—
But when a crime's discovered, then *Macavity's not there!*

He's outwardly respectable. (They say he cheats at cards.)
And his footprints are not found in any file of Scotland Yard's.
And when the larder's looted, or the jewel-case is rifled,
Or when the milk is missing, or another Peke's been stifled,
Or the greenhouse glass is broken, and the trellis past repair—
Ay, there's the wonder of the thing! *Macavity's not there!*

And when the Foreign Office find a Treaty's gone astray,
Or the Admiralty lose some plans and drawings by the way,
There may be a scrap of paper in the hall or on the stair—
But it's useless to investigate—*Macavity's not there!*
And when the loss has been disclosed, the Secret Service say:
"It *must* have been Macavity!"—but he's a mile away.
You'll be sure to find him resting, or a-licking of his thumbs,
Or engaged in doing complicated long division sums.

Macavity, Macavity, there's no one like Macavity,
There never was a Cat of such deceitfulness and suavity.
He always has an alibi, and one or two to spare:
At whatever time the deed took place—MACAVITY WASN'T
        THERE!
And they say that all the Cats whose wicked deeds are widely
        known
(I might mention Mungojerrie, I might mention Griddlebone)
Are nothing more than agents for the Cat who all the time
Just controls their operations: the Napoleon of Crime!

T. S. ELIOT

If—

If you can keep your head when all about you
   Are losing theirs and blaming it on you,
If you can trust yourself when all men doubt you,
   But make allowance for their doubting too;
If you can wait and not be tired by waiting,
   Or being lied about, don't deal in lies,
Or being hated don't give way to hating,
   And yet don't look too good, nor talk too wise:

If you can dream—and not make dreams your master;
   If you can think—and not make thoughts your aim:
If you can meet with Triumph and Disaster
   And treat those two impostors just the same;
If you can bear to hear the truth you've spoken
   Twisted by knaves to make a trap for fools,
Or watch the things you gave your life to, broken,
   And stoop and build 'em up with worn-out tools:

If you can make one heap of all your winnings
   And risk it on one turn of pitch-and-toss,
And lose, and start again at your beginnings
   And never breathe a word about your loss;
If you can force your heart and nerve and sinew
   To serve your turn long after they are gone,
And so hold on when there is nothing in you
   Except the Will which says to them: "Hold on!"

If you can talk with crowds and keep your virtue,
   Or walk with Kings—nor lose the common touch,
If neither foes nor loving friends can hurt you,
   If all men count with you, but none too much;
If you can fill the unforgiving minute
   With sixty seconds' worth of distance run,
Yours is the Earth and everything that's in it,
   And—which is more—you'll be a Man, my son!

RUDYARD KIPLING

The Song of the Mad Prince

Who said, "Peacock Pie"?
  The old King to the sparrow:
Who said, "Crops are ripe"?
  Rust to the harrow:
Who said, "Where sleeps she now?
  Where rests she now her head,
Bathed in eve's loveliness"?—
  That's what I said.

Who said, "Ay, mum's the word"?
  Sexton to willow:
Who said, "Green dusk for dreams,
  Moss for a pillow"?
Who said, "All Time's delight
  Hath she for narrow bed;
Life's troubled bubble broken"?—
  That's what I said.

WALTER DE LA MARE

The Lady of Shalott

Part I

On either side the river lie
Long fields of barley and of rye,
That clothe the wold and meet the sky;
And through the field the road runs by
     To many-towered Camelot;
And up and down the people go,
Gazing where the lilics blow
Round an island there below,
     The island of Shalott.

Willows whiten, aspens quiver,
Little breezes dusk and shiver
Through the wave that runs forever
By the island in the river
     Flowing down to Camelot.
Four gray walls, and four gray towers,
Overlook a space of flowers,
And the silent isle imbowers
     The Lady of Shalott.

By the margin, willow-veiled,
Slide the heavy barges trailed
By slow horses; and unhailed
The shallop flitteth silken-sailed
     Skimming down to Camelot:
But who hath seen her wave her hand?
Or at the casement seen her stand?
Or is she known in all the land,
     The Lady of Shalott?

Only reapers, reaping early
In among the bearded barley,
Hear a song that echoes cheerly
From the river winding clearly,

Down to towered Camelot;
And by the moon the reaper weary,
Piling sheaves in uplands airy,
Listening, whispers, " 'Tis the fairy
    Lady of Shalott."

Part II

There she weaves by night and day
A magic web with colors gay.
She has heard a whisper say,
A curse is on her if she stay
    To look down to Camelot.
She knows not what the curse may be,
And so she weaveth steadily,
And little other care hath she,
    The Lady of Shalott.

And moving through a mirror clear
That hangs before her all the year,
Shadows of the world appear.
There she sees the highway near
    Winding down to Camelot;
There the river eddy whirls,
And there the surly village churls,
And the red cloaks of market girls,
    Pass onward from Shalott.

Sometimes a troop of damsels glad,
An abbot on an ambling pad,
Sometimes a curly shepherd lad,
Or long-haired page in crimson clad,
    Goes by to towered Camelot;
And sometimes through the mirror blue
The knights come riding two and two:
She hath no loyal knight and true,
    The Lady of Shalott.

But in her web she still delights

To weave the mirror's magic sights,
For often through the silent nights
A funeral, with plumes and lights
      And music, went to Camelot;
Or when the moon was overhead,
Came two young lovers lately wed:
"I am half sick of shadows," said
      The Lady of Shalott.

Part III

A bowshot from her bower eaves,
He rode between the barley sheaves,
The sun came dazzling through the leaves,
And flamed upon the brazen greaves
      Of bold Sir Lancelot.
A red-cross knight forever kneeled
To a lady in his shield,
That sparkled on the yellow field,
      Beside remote Shalott.

The gemmy bridle glittered free,
Like to some branch of stars we see
Hung in the golden Galaxy.
The bridle bells rang merrily
      As he rode down to Camelot;
And from his blazoned baldric slung
A mighty silver bugle hung,
And as he rode his armor rung,
      Beside remote Shalott.

All in the blue unclouded weather
Thick-jeweled shone the saddle leather,
The helmet and the helmet-feather
Burned like one burning flame together,
      As he rode down to Camelot;
As often through the purple night,
Below the starry clusters bright,

Some bearded meteor, trailing light,
      Moves over still Shalott.

His broad clear brow in sunlight glowed;
On burnished hooves his war horse trode;
From underneath his helmet flowed
His coal-black curls as on he rode,
      As he rode down to Camelot.
From the bank and from the river
He flashed into the crystal mirror,
"Tirra lirra," by the river
      Sang Sir Lancelot.

She left the web, she left the loom,
She made three paces through the room,
She saw the water lily bloom,
She saw the helmet and the plume,
      She looked down to Camelot.
Out flew the web and floated wide;
The mirror cracked from side to side;
"The curse is come upon me," cried
      The Lady of Shalott.

Part IV

In the stormy east wind straining,
The pale yellow woods were waning,
The broad stream in his banks complaining,
Heavily the low sky raining
      Over towered Camelot;
Down she came and found a boat
Beneath a willow left afloat,
And round about the prow she wrote
      The Lady of Shalott.

And down the river's dim expanse
Like some bold seër in a trance,
Seeing all his own mischance—
With a glassy countenance

Did she look to Camelot.
And at the closing of the day
She loosed the chain, and down she lay;
The broad stream bore her far away,
　　The Lady of Shalott.

Lying, robed in snowy white
That loosely flew to left and right—
The leaves upon her falling light—
Through the noises of the night
　　　　She floated down to Camelot;
And as the boat-head wound along
The willowy hills and fields among,
They heard her singing her last song,
　　The Lady of Shalott.

Heard a carol, mournful, holy,
Chanted loudly, chanted lowly,
Till her blood was frozen slowly,
And her eyes were darkened wholly,
　　　　Turned to towered Camelot.
For ere she reached upon the tide
The first house by the waterside,
Singing in her song she died,
　　The Lady of Shalott.

Under tower and balcony,
By garden wall and gallery,
A gleaming shape she floated by,
Dead-pale between the houses high,
　　　　Silent into Camelot.
Out upon the wharfs they came,
Knight and burgher, lord and dame,
And round the prow they read her name,
　　The Lady of Shalott.

Who is this? and what is here?
And in the lighted palace near
Died the sound of royal cheer;

And they crossed themselves for fear,
 All the knights at Camelot:
But Lancelot mused a little space;
He said, "She has a lovely face;
God in his mercy lend her grace,
 The Lady of Shalott."

ALFRED, LORD TENNYSON

The Owl

Downhill I came, hungry, and yet not starved;
Cold, yet had heat within me that was proof
Against the north wind; tired, yet so that rest
Had seemed the sweetest thing under a roof.

Then at the inn I had food, fire, and rest,
Knowing how hungry, cold, and tired was I.
All of the night was quite barred out except
An owl's cry, a most melancholy cry

Shaken out long and clear upon the hill,
No merry note, nor cause of merriment,
But one telling me plain what I escaped
And others could not, that night, as in I went.

And salted was my food, and my repose,
Salted and sobered, too, by the bird's voice
Speaking for all who lay under the stars,
Soldiers and poor, unable to rejoice.

EDWARD THOMAS

A True Account of Talking to the Sun at Fire Island

The Sun woke me this morning loud
and clear, saying "Hey! I've been
trying to wake you up for fifteen
minutes. Don't be so rude, you are
only the second poet I've ever chosen
to speak to personally

               so why
aren't you more attentive? If I could
burn you through the window I would
to wake you up. I can't hang around
here all day."

              "Sorry, Sun, I stayed
up late last night talking to Hal."

"When I woke up Mayakovsky he was
a lot more prompt" the Sun said
petulantly. "Most people are up
already waiting to see if I'm going
to put in an appearance."

                    I tried
to apologize "I missed you yesterday."
"That's better" he said. "I didn't
know you'd come out." "You may be
wondering why I've come so close?"
"Yes" I said beginning to feel hot
wondering if maybe he wasn't burning me
   anyway.

         "Frankly I wanted to tell you
I like your poetry. I see a lot
on my rounds and you're okay. You may
not be the greatest thing on earth, but
you're different. Now, I've heard some
say you're crazy, they being excessively
calm themselves to my mind, and other
crazy poets think that you're a boring

185

reactionary. Not me.
                        Just keep on
like I do and pay no attention. You'll
find that people always will complain
about the atmosphere, either too hot
or too cold too bright or too dark, days
too short or too long.
                        If you don't appear
at all one day they think you're lazy
or dead. Just keep right on, I like it.

And don't worry about your lineage
poetic or natural. The Sun shines on
the jungle, you know, on the tundra
the sea, the ghetto. Wherever you were
I knew it and saw you moving. I was waiting
for you to get to work.

                        And now that you
are making your own days, so to speak,
even if no one reads you but me
you won't be depressed. Not
everyone can look up, even at me. It
hurts their eyes."
                        "Oh Sun, I'm so grateful to you!"

"Thanks and remember I'm watching. It's
easier for me to speak to you out
here. I don't have to slide down
between buildings to get your ear.
I know you love Manhattan, but
you ought to look up more often.
                                        And
always embrace things, people earth
sky stars, as I do, freely and with
the appropriate sense of space. That
is your inclination, known in the heavens
and you should follow it to hell, if

necessary, which I doubt.

Maybe we'll
speak again in Africa, of which I too
am specially fond. Go back to sleep now
Frank, and I may leave a tiny poem
in that brain of yours as my farewell."

"Sun, don't go!" I was awake
at last. "No, go I must, they're calling
me."

"Who are they?"

Rising he said "Some
day you'll know. They're calling to you
too." Darkly he rose, and then I slept.

FRANK O'HARA

Pete at the Zoo

I wonder if the elephant
Is lonely in his stall
When all the boys and girls are gone
And there's no shout at all,
And there's no one to stamp before,
No one to note his might.
Does he hunch up, as I do,
Against the dark of night?

GWENDOLYN BROOKS

A Visit from St. Nicholas

'Twas the night before Christmas, when all through the house
Not a creature was stirring, not even a mouse;
The stockings were hung by the chimney with care,
In hopes that St. Nicholas soon would be there;
The children were nestled all snug in their beds,
While visions of sugar-plums danced in their heads;
And mamma in her 'kerchief, and I in my cap,
Had just settled our brains for a long winter's nap—
When out on the lawn there arose such a clatter,
I sprang from my bed to see what was the matter.
Away to the window I flew like a flash,
Tore open the shutters and threw up the sash.
The moon, on the breast of the new-fallen snow,
Gave a lustre of midday to objects below;
When, what to my wondering eyes should appear,
But a miniature sleigh and eight tiny reindeer,
With a little old driver, so lively and quick,
I knew in a moment it must be St. Nick.
More rapid than eagles his coursers they came,
And he whistled, and shouted, and called them by name:
"Now, *Dasher!* now, *Dancer!* now, *Prancer* and *Vixen!*
On, *Comet!* on, *Cupid!* on, *Donder* and *Blitzen!*
To the top of the porch! to the top of the wall!
Now dash away! dash away! dash away all!"
As dry leaves that before the wild hurricane fly,
When they meet with an obstacle, mount to the sky,
So up to the house-top the coursers they flew
With the sleigh full of toys, and St. Nicholas too.
And then, in a twinkling, I heard on the roof
The prancing and pawing of each little hoof—
As I drew in my head, and was turning around,
Down the chimney St. Nicholas came with a bound.
He was dressed all in fur, from his head to his foot,
And his clothes were all tarnished with ashes and soot;

A bundle of toys he had flung on his back,
And he looked like a pedlar just opening his pack.
His eyes—how they twinkled; his dimples, how merry!
His cheeks were like roses, his nose like a cherry!
His droll little mouth was drawn up like a bow,
And the beard of his chin was as white as the snow;
The stump of a pipe he held tight in his teeth,
And the smoke it encircled his head like a wreath;
He had a broad face and a little round belly,
That shook when he laughed, like a bowl full of jelly.
He was chubby and plump, a right jolly old elf,
And I laughed when I saw him, in spite of myself.
A wink of his eye and a twist of his head
Soon gave me to know I had nothing to dread;
He spoke not a word, but went straight to his work,
And filled all the stockings; then turned with a jerk,
And laying his finger aside of his nose,
And giving a nod, up the chimney he rose;
He sprang to his sleigh, to his team gave a whistle,
And away they all flew like the down of a thistle.
But I heard him exclaim, ere he drove out of sight,
"Happy Christmas to all, and to all a good night!"

CLEMENT CLARKE MOORE

Flint

An emerald is as green as grass,
  A ruby red as blood;
A sapphire shines as blue as heaven;
  A flint lies in the mud.

A diamond is a brilliant stone,
  To catch the world's desire;
An opal holds a fiery spark;
  But a flint holds fire.

CHRISTINA ROSSETTI

Afton Water

Flow gently, sweet Afton, among thy green braes,
Flow gently, I'll sing thee a song in thy praise;
My Mary's asleep by thy murmuring stream,
Flow gently, sweet Afton, disturb not her dream.

Thou stock-dove whose echo resounds through the glen,
Ye wild whistling blackbirds in yon thorny den,
Thou green-crested lapwing, thy screaming forbear,
I charge you disturb not my slumbering fair.

How lofty, sweet Afton, thy neighboring hills,
Far marked with the courses of clear winding rills;
There daily I wander as noon rises high,
My flocks and my Mary's sweet cot in my eye.

How pleasant thy banks and green valleys below,
Where wild in the woodlands the primroses blow;
There oft as mild evening weeps over the lea,
The sweet-scented birk shades my Mary and me.

Thy crystal stream, Afton, how lovely it glides,
And winds by the cot where my Mary resides;
How wanton thy waters her snowy feet lave,
As gathering sweet flowerets she stems thy clear wave.

Flow gently, sweet Afton, among thy green braes,
Flow gently, sweet river, the theme of my lays;
My Mary's asleep by thy murmuring stream,
Flow gently, sweet Afton, disturb not her dream.

ROBERT BURNS

Song

When I am dead, my dearest,
  Sing no sad songs for me;
Plant thou no roses at my head,
  Nor shady cypress tree.
Be the green grass above me
  With showers and dewdrops wet;
And if thou wilt, remember,
  And if thou wilt, forget.

I shall not see the shadows,
  I shall not feel the rain;
I shall not hear the nightingale
  Sing on as if in pain.
And dreaming through the twilight
  That doth not rise nor set,
Haply I may remember,
  And haply may forget.

CHRISTINA ROSSETTI

Where Go the Boats?

Dark brown is the river,
   Golden is the sand;
It flows along forever,
   With trees on either hand.

Green leaves a-floating,
   Castles of the foam,
Boats of mine a-boating—
   Where will all come home?

On goes the river
   And out past the mill,
Away down the valley,
   Away down the hill.

Away down the river,
   A hundred miles or more,
Other little children
   Shall bring my boats ashore.

ROBERT LOUIS STEVENSON

in Just-
spring   when the world is mud-
luscious the little
lame balloonman

whistles   far   and wee

and eddieandbill come
running from marbles and
piracies and it's
spring

when the world is puddle-wonderful

the queer
old balloonman whistles
far   and   wee
and bettyandisbel come dancing

from hop-scotch and jump-rope and

it's
spring
and
      the
            goat-footed

balloonMan   whistles
far
and
wee

E. E. CUMMINGS

Journey of the Magi

"A cold coming we had of it,
Just the worst time of the year
For a journey, and such a long journey:
The ways deep and the weather sharp,
The very dead of winter."
And the camels galled, sore-footed, refractory,
Lying down in the melting snow.
There were times we regretted
The summer palaces on slopes, the terraces,
And the silken girls bringing sherbet.
Then the camel men cursing and grumbling
And running away, and wanting their liquor and women,
And the night-fires going out, and the lack of shelters,
And the cities hostile and the towns unfriendly
And the villages dirty and charging high prices:
A hard time we had of it.
At the end we preferred to travel all night,
Sleeping in snatches,
With the voices singing in our ears, saying
That this was all folly.

Then at dawn we came down to a temperate valley,
Wet, below the snow line, smelling of vegetation;
With a running stream and a water-mill beating the darkness,
And three trees on the low sky,
And an old white horse galloped away in the meadow.
Then we came to a tavern with vine-leaves over the lintel,
Six hands at an open door dicing for pieces of silver,
And feet kicking the empty wine-skins.
But there was no information, and so we continued
And arrived at evening, not a moment too soon
Finding the place; it was (you may say) satisfactory.

All this was a long time ago, I remember,
And I would do it again, but set down

This set down
This: were we led all that way for
Birth or Death? There was a Birth, certainly,
We had evidence and no doubt. I had seen birth and death,
But had thought they were different; this Birth was
Hard and bitter agony for us, like Death, our death.
We returned to our places, these Kingdoms,
But no longer at ease here, in the old dispensation,
With an alien people clutching their gods.
I should be glad of another death.

T. S. ELIOT

Winter

When icicles hang by the wall,
    And Dick the shepherd blows his nail,
And Tom bears logs into the hall,
    And milk comes frozen home in pail,
When blood is nipp'd, and ways be foul,
Then nightly sings the staring owl,
        Tu-whit, to-who,
        A merry note,
While greasy Joan doth keel the pot.

When all aloud the wind doth blow,
    And coughing drowns the parson's saw,
And birds sit brooding in the snow,
    And Marian's nose looks red and raw,
When roasted crabs hiss in the bowl,
Then nightly sings the staring owl,
        Tu-whit, to-who,
        A merry note,
While greasy Joan doth keel the pot.

WILLIAM SHAKESPEARE

Song From "Pippa Passes"

The year's at the spring
And day's at the morn;
Morning's at seven;
The hill-side's dew-pearled;
The lark's on the wing;
The snail's on the thorn:
God's in his heaven—
All's right with the world!

ROBERT BROWNING

The Old Man's Comforts
and How He Gained Them

You are old, father William, the young man cried,
  The few locks which are left you are gray;
You are hale, father William, a hearty old man,
  Now tell me the reason, I pray.

In the days of my youth, father William replied,
  I remember'd that youth would fly fast,
And abused not my health and my vigor at first,
  That I never might need them at last.

You are old, father William, the young man cried,
  And pleasures with youth pass away;
And yet you lament not the days that are gone,
  Now tell me the reason, I pray.

In the days of my youth, father William replied,
  I remember'd that youth could not last;
I thought of the future, whatever I did,
  That I never might grieve for the past.

You are old, father William, the young man cried,
  And life must be hastening away;
You are cheerful, and love to converse upon death,
  Now tell me the reason, I pray.

I am cheerful, young man, father William replied,
  Let the cause thy attention engage;
In the days of my youth I remember'd my God!
  And He hath not forgotten my age.

ROBERT SOUTHEY

200

You Are Old, Father William

"You are old, father William," the young man said,
　"And your hair has become very white;
And yet you incessantly stand on your head—
　Do you think, at your age, it is right?"

"In my youth," father William replied to his son,
　"I feared it might injure the brain;
But now that I'm perfectly sure I have none,
　Why, I do it again and again."

"You are old," said the youth, "as I mentioned before,
　And have grown most uncommonly fat;
Yet you turned a back-somersault in at the door—
　Pray what is the reason for that?"

"In my youth," said the sage, as he shook his gray locks,
　"I kept all my limbs very supple
By the use of this ointment—one shilling the box—
　Allow me to sell you a couple?"

"You are old," said the youth, "and your jaws are too weak
　For anything tougher than suet;
Yet you finished the goose, with the bones and the beak—
　Pray, how did you manage to do it?"

"In my youth," said his father, "I took to the law,
　And argued each case with my wife;
And the muscular strength which it gave to my jaw
　Has lasted the rest of my life."

"You are old," said the youth, "one would hardly suppose
　That your eye was as steady as ever;
Yet you balanced an eel on the end of your nose—
　What made you so awfully clever?"

"I have answered three questions and that is enough,"
  Said his father. "Don't give yourself airs!
Do you think I can listen all day to such stuff?
  Be off, or I'll kick you downstairs!"

LEWIS CARROLL

Jabberwocky

'Twas brillig, and the slithy toves
  Did gyre and gimble in the wabe:
All mimsy were the borogoves,
    And the mome raths outgrabe.

"Beware the Jabberwock, my son!
  The jaws that bite, the claws that catch!
Beware the Jubjub bird, and shun
    The frumious Bandersnatch!"

He took his vorpal sword in hand:
  Long time the manxome foe he sought—
So rested he by the Tumtum tree,
    And stood awhile in thought.

And, as in uffish thought he stood,
  The Jabberwock, with eyes of flame,
Came whiffling through the tulgey wood,
    And burbled as it came!

One, two! One, two! And through and through
  The vorpal blade went snicker-snack!
He left it dead, and with its head
    He went galumphing back.

"And hast thou slain the Jabberwock?
  Come to my arms, my beamish boy!
O frabjous day! Callooh! Callay!"
    He chortled in his joy.

'Twas brillig, and the slithy toves
  Did gyre and gimble in the wabe:
All mimsy were the borogoves,
    And the mome raths outgrabe.

LEWIS CARROLL

still
it was nice
when the scissors man come round
running his wheel
rolling his wheel
and the sparks shooting
out in the dark
across the lot
and over to the white folks section

still
it was nice
in the light of Maizie's store
to watch the wheel
and catch the wheel—
fire spinning in the air
and our edges
and our points
sharpening good as anybodys'

LUCILLE CLIFTON

The King of Yvetot

There was a king of Yvetot,
  Of whom renown hath little said,
Who let all thoughts of glory go,
  And dawdled half his days a-bed;
And every night, as night came round,
By Jenny, with a nightcap crowned,
    Slept very sound.
  Sing ho, ho, ho! and he, he, he!
  That's the kind of king for me.

And every day it came to pass
  That four lusty meals made he;
And, step by step, upon an ass,
  Rode abroad, his realms to see;
And wherever he did stir,
What think you was his escort, sir?
    Why, an old cur.
  Sing ho, ho, ho! and he, he, he!
  That's the kind of king for me.

To all the ladies of the land,
  A courteous king, and kind, was he;
The reason why you'll understand,
  They named him *Pater Patriae.*
Each year he called his fighting men
And marched a league from home, and then
    Marched back again.
  Sing ho, ho, ho! and he, he, he!
  That's the kind of king for me.

The portrait of this best of kings
  Is standing still, upon a sign
That on a village tavern swings,
  Famed in the country for good wine.
The people in their Sunday trim,
Filling their glasses to the brim,

Look up to him,
Singing ho, ho, ho! and he, he, he!
That's the kind of king for me.

WILLIAM MAKEPEACE THACKERAY

Good Times

My Daddy has paid the rent
and the insurance man is gone
and the lights is back on
and my uncle Brud has hit
for one dollar straight
and they is good times
good times
good times

My Mama has made bread
and Grampaw has come
and everybody is drunk
and dancing in the kitchen
and singing in the kitchen
oh these is good times
good times
good times

oh children think about the
good times

LUCILLE CLIFTON

"o purple finch
                please tell me why
this summer world (and you and i
who love so much to live)
                must die"

"if i
   should tell you anything"
(that eagerly sweet carolling
self answers me)
                "i could not sing"

E. E. CUMMINGS

The Tarantula

Everyone thinks I am poisonous. I am not.
Look up and read the authorities on me, especially
One Alexander Petrunkevitch, of Yale, now retired,
Who has said of me (and I quote): my "bite is dangerous
Only
To insects and small mammals such as mice."
I would have you notice that "only"; that is important,
As you who are neither insect nor mouse can appreciate.
I have to live as you do,
And how would you like it if someone construed your relations
With the chicken, say, as proof of your propensities?
Furthermore,
Petrunkevitch has observed, and I can vouch for it,
That I am myopic, lonely and retiring. When I am born
I dig a burrow for me, and me alone,
And live in it all my life except when I come
Up for food and love (in my case the latter
Is not really satisfactory: I
"Wander about after dark in search of females,
And occasionally stray into houses," after which I
Die). How does that sound?
Furthermore,
I have to cope with the digger wasp of the genus
Pepsis; and despite my renown as a killer (nonsense, of course),
I can't. Petrunkevitch says so.
Read him. He's good on the subject. He's helped *me*.

Which brings me to my point here. You carry
This image about of me that is at once libelous
And discouraging, all because you, who should know better,
Find me ugly. So I am ugly. Does that mean that you
Should persecute me as you do? Read William Blake.
Read William Wordsworth.
Read Williams in general, I'd say. There was a book
By a William Tarantula once, a work of some consequence

In my world on the subject of beauty,
Beauty that's skin deep only, beauty that some
Charles (note the "Charles") of the Ritz can apply and take off
At will, beauty that—
                    but I digress.
What I am getting at
Is that you who are blessed (I have read) with understanding
Should understand me, little me. My name is William
Too.

REED WHITTEMORE

Bonny George Campbell

High upon Highlands
    And low upon Tay,
Bonny George Campbell
    Rade out on a day.

Saddled and bridled
    And gallant rade he:
Hame cam his guid horse,
    But never cam he.

Out cam his auld mither.
    Greeting fu' sair,
And out cam his bonny bride,
    Riving her hair.

Saddled and bridled
    And booted rade he:
Toom hame cam the saddle,
    But never cam he.

"My meadow lies green,
    And my corn is unshorn,
My barn is to build,
    And my babe is unborn."

Saddled and bridled
    And booted rade he;
Toom hame cam the saddle,
    But never cam he.

ANONYMOUS

To the Thawing Wind

Come with rain, O loud Southwester!
Bring the singer, bring the nester;
Give the buried flower a dream;
Make the settled snowbank steam;
Find the brown beneath the white;
But whate'er you do tonight,
Bathe my window, make it flow,
Melt it as the ice will go;
Melt the glass and leave the sticks
Like a hermit's crucifix;
Burst into my narrow stall;
Swing the picture on the wall;
Run the rattling pages o'er;
Scatter poems on the floor;
Turn the poet out of door!

ROBERT FROST

Papa Love Baby

My mother was a romantic girl
So she had to marry a man with his hair in curl
Who subsequently became my unrespected papa,
But that was a long time ago now.

What folly it is that daughters are always supposed to be
In love with papa. It wasn't the case with me
I couldn't take to him at all
But he took to me
What a sad fate to befall
A child of three.

I sat upright in my baby carriage
And wished mama hadn't made such a foolish marriage.
I tried to hide it, but it showed in my eyes unfortunately
And a fortnight later papa ran away to sea.

He used to come home on leave
It was always the same
I could not grieve
But I think I was somewhat to blame.

STEVIE SMITH

213

Go to the Shine That's on a Tree

Go to the shine that's on a tree
When dawn has laved with liquid light
With luminous light the nighted tree
And take that glory without fright.

Go to the song that's in a bird
When he has seen the glistening tree,
That glorious tree the bird has heard
Give praise for its felicity.

Then go to the earth and touch it keen,
Be tree and bird, be wide aware
Be wild aware of light unseen,
And unheard song along the air.

RICHARD EBERHART

A Birthday

My heart is like a singing bird
    Whose nest is in a watered shoot;
My heart is like an apple tree
    Whose boughs are bent with thickset fruit;
My heart is like a rainbow shell
    That paddles in a halcyon sea;
My heart is gladder than all these
    Because my love is come to me.

Raise me a dais of silk and down;
    Hang it with vair and purple dyes;
Carve it in doves and pomegranates,
    And peacocks with a hundred eyes;
Work it in gold and silver grapes,
    In leaves and silver fleurs-de-lys;
Because the birthday of my life
    Is come, my love is come to me.

CHRISTINA ROSSETTI

The Brook

I come from haunts of coot and hern,
  I make a sudden sally
And sparkle out among the fern,
  To bicker down a valley.

By thirty hills I hurry down,
  Or slip between the ridges,
By twenty thorps, a little town,
  And half a hundred bridges.

Till last by Philip's farm I flow
  To join the brimming river,
For men may come and men may go,
  But I go on for ever.

I chatter over stony ways,
  In little sharps and trebles,
I bubble into eddying bays,
  I babble on the pebbles.

With many a curve my banks I fret
  By many a field and fallow,
And many a fairy foreland set
  With willow-weed and mallow.

I chatter, chatter, as I flow
  To join the brimming river,
For men may come and men may go,
  But I go on for ever.

I wind about, and in and out,
  With here a blossom sailing,
And here and there a lusty trout,
  And here and there a grayling,

And here and there a foamy flake
  Upon me, as I travel
With many a silvery waterbreak
  Above the golden gravel.

And draw them all along, and flow
  To join the brimming river,
For men may come and men may go,
  But I go on for ever.

I steal by lawns and grassy plots,
  I slide by hazel covers;
I move the sweet forget-me-nots
  That grow for happy lovers.

I slip, I slide, I gloom, I glance,
  Among my skimming swallows;
I make the netted sunbeam dance
  Against my sandy shallows.

I murmur under moon and stars
  In brambly wildernesses;
I linger by my shingly bars;
  I loiter round my cresses;

And out again I curve and flow
  To join the brimming river,
For men may come and men may go,
  But I go on for ever.

ALFRED, LORD TENNYSON

The Runaway

Once when the snow of the year was beginning to fall,
We stopped by a mountain pasture to say, "Whose colt?"
A little Morgan had one forefoot on the wall,
The other curled at his breast. He dipped his head
And snorted at us. And then he had to bolt.
We heard the miniature thunder where he fled,
And we saw him, or thought we saw him, dim and gray,
Like a shadow against the curtain of falling flakes.
"I think the little fellow's afraid of the snow.
He isn't winter-broken. It isn't play
With the little fellow at all. He's running away.
I doubt if even his mother could tell him, 'Sakes,
It's only weather.' He'd think she didn't know!
Where is his mother? He can't be out alone."
And now he comes again with clatter of stone,
And mounts the wall again with whited eyes
And all his tail that isn't hair up straight.
He shudders his coat as if to throw off flies.
"Whoever it is that leaves him out so late,
When other creatures have gone to stall and bin,
Ought to be told to come and take him in."

ROBERT FROST

To an Athlete Dying Young

The time you won your town the race
We chaired you through the market-place;
Man and boy stood cheering by,
And home we brought you shoulder-high.

Today, the road all runners come,
Shoulder-high we bring you home,
And set you at your threshold down,
Townsman of a stiller town.

Smart lad, to slip betimes away
From fields where glory does not stay,
And early though the laurel grows
It withers quicker than the rose.

Eyes the shady night has shut
Cannot see the record cut,
And silence sounds no worse than cheers
After earth has stopped the ears:

Now you will not swell the rout
Of lads that wore their honors out,
Runners whom renown outran
And the name died before the man.

So set, before its echoes fade,
The fleet foot on the sill of shade,
And hold to the low lintel up
The still-defended challenge-cup.

And round that early-laureled head
Will flock to gaze the strengthless dead,
And find unwithered on its curls
The garland briefer than a girl's.

A. E. HOUSMAN

The Jumblies

They went to sea in a sieve, they did;
  In a sieve they went to sea;
In spite of all their friends could say,
On a winter's morn, on a stormy day,
  In a sieve they went to sea.
And when the sieve turned round and round,
And everyone cried, "You'll be drowned!"
They called aloud, "Our sieve ain't big,
But we don't care a button; we don't care a fig—
  In a sieve we'll go to sea!"
    Far and few, far and few,
      Are the lands where the Jumblies live.
      Their heads are green, and their hands are blue;
      And they went to sea in a sieve.

They sailed away in a sieve, they did,
  In a sieve they sailed so fast,
With only a beautiful pea-green veil
Tied with a ribbon, by way of a sail,
  To a small tobacco-pipe mast.
And everyone said who saw them go,
"Oh! won't they be soon upset, you know,
For the sky is dark, and the voyage is long;
And, happen what may, it's extremely wrong
  In a sieve to sail so fast."

The water it soon came in, it did;
  The water it soon came in.
So, to keep them dry, they wrapped their feet
In a pinky paper all folded neat;
  And they fastened it down with a pin.
And they passed the night in a crockery-jar;
And each of them said, "How wise we are!
Though the sky be dark, and the voyage be long,
Yet we never can think we were rash or wrong,
  While round in our sieve we spin."

And all night long they sailed away;
   And, when the sun went down,
They whistled and warbled a moony song
To the echoing sound of a coppery gong,
   In the shade of the mountains brown,
"O Timballoo! how happy we are
When we live in a sieve and a crockery-jar!
And all night long, in the moonlight pale,
We sail away with a pea-green sail
   In the shade of the mountains brown."

They sailed to the Western Sea, they did—
   To a land all covered with trees;
And they bought an owl, and a useful cart,
And a pound of rice, and a cranberry-tart,
   And a hive of silvery bees;
And they bought a pig, and some green jackdaws,
And a lovely monkey with lollipop paws,
And seventeen bags of edelweiss tea,
And forty bottles of ring-bo-ree,
   And no end of Stilton cheese.

And in twenty years they all came back—
   In twenty years or more;
And everyone said, "How tall they've grown!
For they've been to the Lakes, and the Torrible Zone,
   And the hills of the Chankly Bore."
And they drank their health, and gave them a feast
Of dumplings made of beautiful yeast;
And everyone said, "If we only live,
We, too, will go to sea in a sieve,
   To the hills of the Chankly Bore."
      Far and few, far and few,
         Are the lands where the Jumblies live.
      Their heads are green, and their hands are blue;
         And they went to sea in a sieve.

EDWARD LEAR

Cruel Jenny Wren

Jenny Wren fell sick,
    Upon a merry time.
In came Robin-Redbreast
    And brought her sops and wine.

"Eat well of the sops, Jenny,
    Drink well of the wine."
"Thank you, Robin, kindly,
    You shall be mine."

Jenny she got well,
    And stood upon her feet,
And told Robin plainly,
    She loved him not a bit.

Robin, being angry,
    Hopped upon a twig,
Saying, "Out upon you! Fie upon you!
    Bold-faced jig!"

ANONYMOUS

Poppies in October

Even the sun-clouds this morning cannot manage such skirts.
Nor the woman in the ambulance
Whose red heart blooms through her coat so astoundingly——

A gift, a love gift
Utterly unasked for
By a sky

Palely and flamily
Igniting its carbon monoxides, by eyes
Dulled to a halt under bowlers.

O my God, what am I
That these late mouths should cry open
In a forest of frost, in a dawn of cornflowers.

SYLVIA PLATH

The Wraggle Taggle Gypsies

There were three gypsies a-come to my door,
And down-stairs ran this a-lady, O!
One sang high, and another sang low,
And the other sang, Bonny, bonny Biscay, O!

Then she pulled off her silk-finished gown
And put on hose of leather, O!
The ragged, ragged rags about our door—
She's gone with the wraggle taggle gypsies, O!

It was late last night, when my lord came home,
Enquiring for his a-lady, O!
The servants said, on every hand:
"She's gone with the wraggle taggle gypsies, O!"

"O saddle to me my milk-white steed,
Go and fetch me my pony, O!
That I may ride and seek my bride,
Who is gone with the wraggle taggle gypsies, O!"

O he rode high and he rode low,
He rode through woods and copses too,
Until he came to an open field,
And there he espied his a-lady, O!

"What makes you leave your house and land?
What makes you leave your money, O?
What makes you leave your new-wedded lord;
To go with the wraggle taggle gypsies, O!"

"What care I for my house and my land?
What care I for my money, O?
What care I for my new-wedded lord?
I'm off with the wraggle taggle gypsies, O!"

"Last night you slept on a goose-feather bed,
With the sheet turned down so bravely, O!
And to-night you'll sleep in a cold open field,
Along with the wraggle taggle gypsies, O!"

"What care I for a goose-feather bed,
With the sheet turned down so bravely, O?
For to-night I shall sleep in a cold open field,
Along with the wraggle taggle gypsies, O!"

ANONYMOUS

Sales Talk for Annie

Eat your banana, Annie dear;
   It's from a tropic tree
In lands where lurked the buccaneer
   By the Río Tilirí,
Or where the Cockscomb Mountains rise
   Above the Monkey River,
And lonely men with fevered eyes
   By turns perspire and shiver.
The parrot and the kinkajou
   And the armor-clad iguana
Have spared this golden fruit for you—
   But no, she won't even touch the lovely banana!

Eat your tapioca, please.
   In forests of Brazil
The Tupis and the Guaranis
   Have cooked it on a grill.
The poison of cassava roots
   Is thereby circumvented,
And flour and bread it constitutes.
   (It often is fermented.)
From Urubú and Urucú
   To distant Yanaoca
Indians grew this food for you,
   So for gosh sakes get going on your tapioca.

Drink your milk, my little lass.
   Oh, does it not look yummy!
A moo-cow ate the sun-lit grass
   And made it in her tummy.
The moo-cow's milk is free from faults,
   It's good for every human
(Containing sugar, fats, and salts,
   And casein and albumin.)
Here, I said to drink it, not blow in it! Listen, Annie,

How would you like to have Father take that glass of milk
  and ram it
Down your throat? How would you like a good swift whack on
  the fanny?
All right, go ahead and cry, damn it!

MORRIS BISHOP

"The Ousel Cock"—

I asked a cock blackbird,
"Why did you choose black?
"—In the ages of old
"When blackbirds were new
"And questions of hue
"Began to unfold—
"With the rainbow to choose from,
"Why did you pick black?"

"You mean," he replied,
"That a blackbird's no posy . . .
"But that point aside;
"This charge that we slighted
"The rainbow of old:
"Are you nearsighted?
—"Black goes with gold
"In a manner that dizzies
"Our hens to behold
"In the Spring of the year;
"That's why we chose black
"In the ages far back,
"And how we got here,
"If you need to be told."

RALPH HODGSON

Snow in the Suburbs

Every branch big with it,
Bent every twig with it;
Every fork like a white web-foot;
Every street and pavement mute:
Some flakes have lost their way, and grope back upward, when
Meeting those meandering down they turn and descend again.
The palings are glued together like a wall,
And there is no waft of wind with the fleecy fall.

A sparrow enters the tree,
Whereon immediately
A snow-lump thrice his own slight size
Descends on him and showers his head and eyes,
And overturns him,
And near inurns him,
And lights on a nether twig, when its brush
Starts off a volley of other lodging lumps with a rush.

The steps are a blanched slope,
Up which, with feeble hope,
A black cat comes, wide-eyed and thin;
And we take him in.

THOMAS HARDY

The Song of the Old Mother

I rise in the dawn, and I kneel and blow
Till the seed of the fire flicker and glow;
And then I must scrub and bake and sweep
Till stars are beginning to blink and peep;
And the young lie long and dream in their bed
Of the matching of ribbons for bosom and head,
And their day goes over in idleness,
And they sigh if the wind but lift a tress:
While I must work because I am old,
And the seed of the fire gets feeble and cold.

WILLIAM BUTLER YEATS

The Gallows

There was a weasel lived in the sun
With all his family,
Till a keeper shot him with his gun
And hung him up on a tree,
Where he swings in the wind and rain,
In the sun and in the snow,
Without pleasure, without pain,
On the dead oak tree bough.

There was a crow who was no sleeper,
But a thief and a murderer
Till a very late hour; and this keeper
Made him one of the things that were,
To hang and flap in rain and wind,
In the sun and in the snow.
There are no more sins to be sinned
On the dead oak tree bough.

There was a magpie, too,
Had a long tongue and a long tail;
He could both talk and do—
But what did that avail?
He, too, flaps in the wind and rain
Alongside weasel and crow,
Without pleasure, without pain,
On the dead oak tree bough.

And many other beasts
And birds, skin, bone, and feather,
Have been taken from their feasts
And hung up there together,
To swing and have endless leisure
In the sun and in the snow,
Without pain, without pleasure,
On the dead oak tree bough.

EDWARD THOMAS

In Minako Wada's House

In old Minako Wada's house
Everything has its place,
And mostly out of sight:
 Bedding folded away
 All day, brought down
 From the shelf at night,

Tea things underneath
Low tea table and tablecloth—
And sliding screen doors,
 Landscape-painted, that hide
 Her clothes inside a wash
 Of mountains. Here, the floors

Are a clean-fitting mosaic,
Mats of a texture like
A broom's; and in a niche
 In the tearoom wall
 Is a shrine to all of her
 Ancestors, before which

She sets each day
A doll-sized cup of tea,
A doll-sized bowl of rice.
 She keeps a glass jar
 Of crickets that are fed fish
 Shavings, an eggplant slice,

And whose hushed chorus,
Like the drowsy toss
Of a baby's rattle, moves in
 On so tranquil a song
 It's soon no longer heard.
 The walls are thin

In Minako Wada's little house,
Open to every lifting voice
On the street—by day, the cries
    Of the children, at night
    Those excited, sweet,
    Reiterated goodbyes

Of men full of beer who now
Must hurry home. Just to
Wake in the night inside this nest,
    Late, the street asleep (day done,
    Day not yet begun), is what
    Perhaps she loves best.

                    BRAD LEITHAUSER

The Spider and the Fly

"Will you walk into my parlor?" said the Spider to the Fly,
" 'Tis the prettiest little parlor that ever you did spy;
The way into my parlor is up a winding stair,
And I have many curious things to show when you are there."
"Oh no, no," said the little Fly, "to ask me is in vain,
For who goes up your winding stair can ne'er come down
   again."

"I'm sure you must be weary, dear, with soaring up so high;
Will you rest upon my little bed?" said the Spider to the Fly.
"There are pretty curtains drawn around, the sheets are fine and
   thin;
And if you like to rest awhile, I'll snugly tuck you in!"
"Oh no, no," said the little Fly, "for I've often heard it said,
They never, never wake again, who sleep upon your bed!"

Said the cunning Spider to the Fly, "Dear friend, what can I
   do,
To prove the warm affection I've always felt for you?
I have within my pantry good store of all that's nice;
I'm sure you're very welcome—will you please to take a slice?"
"Oh no, no," said the little Fly, "kind sir, that cannot be,
I've heard what's in your pantry, and I do not wish to see."

"Sweet creature," said the Spider, "you're witty and you're wise;
How handsome are your gauzy wings, how brilliant are your
   eyes!
I have a little looking-glass upon my parlor shelf,
If you'll step in one moment, dear, you shall behold yourself."
"I thank you, gentle sir," she said, "for what you're pleased to
   say,
And bidding you good morning now, I'll call another day."

The Spider turned him round about, and went into his den,
For well he knew the silly Fly would soon come back again.
So he wove a subtle web, in a little corner sly,

And set his table ready, to dine upon the Fly.
Then he came out to his door again, and merrily did sing,
"Come hither, hither, pretty Fly, with the pearl and silver wing;
Your robes are green and purple—there's a crest upon your
    head;
Your eyes are like the diamond bright, but mine are dull as
    lead."

Alas, alas! how very soon this silly little Fly,
Hearing his wily, flattering words, came slowly flitting by;
With buzzing wings she hung aloft, then near and nearer drew,
Thinking only of her brilliant eyes, and green and purple hue;
Thinking only of her crested head—poor foolish thing! At last,
Up jumped the cunning Spider, and fiercely held her fast.
He dragged her up his winding stair, into his dismal den,
Within his little parlor—but she ne'er came out again!

And now, dear little children, who may this story read,
To idle, silly, flattering words, I pray you ne'er give heed;
Unto an evil counsellor, close heart, and ear, and eye,
And take a lesson from this tale, of the Spider and the Fly.

MARY HOWITT

Little Trotty Wagtail

Little trotty wagtail, he went in the rain,
And twittering, tottering sideways he ne'er got straight again.
He stooped to get a worm, and looked up to get a fly,
And then he flew away ere his feathers they were dry.

Little trotty wagtail, he waddled in the mud,
And left his little footmarks, trample where he would.
He waddled in the water-pudge, and waggle went his tail,
And chirrupt up his wings to dry upon the garden rail.

Little trotty wagtail, you nimble all about,
And in the dimpling water-pudge you waddle in and out;
Your home is nigh at hand, and in the warm pig-stye,
So, little Master Wagtail, I'll bid you a good-by.

JOHN CLARE

Sarah Cynthia Sylvia Stout Would Not Take the Garbage Out

Sarah Cynthia Sylvia Stout
Would not take the garbage out!
She'd scour the pots and scrape the pans,
Candy the yams and spice the hams,
And though her daddy would scream and shout,
She simply would not take the garbage out.
And so it piled up to the ceilings:
Coffee grounds, potato peelings,
Brown bananas, rotten peas,
Chunks of sour cottage cheese.
It filled the can, it covered the floor,
It cracked the window and blocked the door
With bacon rinds and chicken bones,
Drippy ends of ice cream cones,
Prune pits, peach pits, orange peel,
Gloppy glumps of cold oatmeal,
Pizza crusts and withered greens,
Soggy beans and tangerines,
Crusts of black burned buttered toast,
Gristly bits of beefy roasts . . .
The garbage rolled on down the hall,
It raised the roof, it broke the wall . . .
Greasy napkins, cookie crumbs,
Globs of gooey bubble gum,
Cellophane from green baloney,
Rubbery blubbery macaroni,
Peanut butter, caked and dry,
Curdled milk and crusts of pie,
Moldy melons, dried-up mustard,
Eggshells mixed with lemon custard,
Cold french fries and rancid meat,
Yellow lumps of Cream of Wheat.
At last the garbage reached so high

That finally it touched the sky.
And all the neighbors moved away,
And none of her friends would come to play.
And finally Sarah Cynthia Stout said,
"OK, I'll take the garbage out!"
But then, of course, it was too late . . .
The garbage reached across the state,
From New York to the Golden Gate.
And there, in the garbage she did hate,
Poor Sarah met an awful fate,
That I cannot right now relate
Because the hour is much too late.
But children, remember Sarah Stout
And always take the garbage out!

SHEL SILVERSTEIN

Autumn Piece

Baffled
by the choreography of the season
the eye could not
with certainty see
whether it was wind
stripping the leaves or
the leaves were struggling to be free:

They came at you
in decaying spirals
plucked flung and regathered by the same
force that was twisting
the scarves of the vapor trails
dragging all certainties out of course:

As the car resisted it
you felt it in either hand
commanding car, tree, sky,
master of chances,
and at a curve was a red
board said "Danger":
I thought it said dancer.

CHARLES TOMLINSON

The Echoing Green

The Sun does arise,
And make happy the skies;
The merry bells ring
To welcome the Spring;
The skylark and thrush,
The birds of the bush,
Sing louder around
To the bells' cheerful sound
While our sports shall be seen
On the Echoing Green.

Old John, with white hair,
Does laugh away care,
Sitting under the oak,
Among the old folk.
They laugh at our play,
And soon they all say:
"Such, such were the joys
When we all, girls and boys,
In our youth time were seen
On the Echoing Green."

Till the little ones, weary,
No more can be merry;
The sun does descend,
And our sports have an end.
Round the laps of their mothers
Many sisters and brothers,
Like birds in their nest,
Are ready for rest,
And sport no more seen
On the darkening Green.

WILLIAM BLAKE

The Cow

The friendly cow all red and white,
   I love with all my heart:
She gives me cream with all her might,
   To eat with apple-tart.

She wanders lowing here and there,
   And yet she cannot stray,
All in the pleasant open air,
   The pleasant light of day.

And blown by all the winds that pass
   And wet with all the showers,
She walks among the meadow grass
   And eats the meadow flowers.

ROBERT LOUIS STEVENSON

A Kitten's Thought

It's very nice to think of how
In every country lives a Cow
To furnish milk with all her might
For Kitten's comfort and delight.

OLIVER HERFORD

Jephson Gardens

Two small children in the Gardens on Sunday,
Playing quietly at husband and wife.

How sweet, says an old lady, as she sits on
The bench: you must surely be brother and sister?

No, says the boy, we are husband and wife.
How sweet, says the old lady: but really you are
Brother and sister, aren't you now, really?

No, says the boy, trapped in his fantasy,
I am the husband, she is the wife.

The old lady moves off, she doesn't like liars,
She says. She doesn't think we are sweet any longer.

D. J. ENRIGHT

Wynken, Blynken, and Nod

Wynken, Blynken, and Nod one night
   Sailed off in a wooden shoe—
Sailed on a river of crystal light,
   Into a sea of dew.
"Where are you going, and what do you wish?"
   The old moon asked the three.
"We have come to fish for the herring fish
   That live in this beautiful sea;
   Nets of silver and gold have we!"
        Said Wynken,
        Blynken,
        And Nod.

The old moon laughed and sang a song,
   As they rocked in the wooden shoe,
And the wind that sped them all night long
   Ruffled the waves of dew.
The little stars were the herring fish
   That lived in that beautiful sea—
"Now cast your nets wherever you wish
   Never afeared are we";
So cried the stars to the fishermen three:
        Wynken,
        Blynken,
        And Nod.

All night long their nets they threw
   To the stars in the twinkling foam—
Then down from the skies came the wooden shoe,
   Bringing the fishermen home;
'Twas all so pretty a sail it seemed
   As if it could not be,
And some folks thought 'twas a dream they'd dreamed
Of sailing that beautiful sea—

But I shall name you the fishermen three:
> Wynken,
> Blynken,
> And Nod.

Wynken and Blynken are two little eyes,
> And Nod is a little head,
And the wooden shoe that sailed the skies
> Is a wee one's trundle-bed.
So shut your eyes while mother sings
> Of wonderful sights that be,
And you shall see the beautiful things
> As you rock in the misty sea,
> Where the old shoe rocked the fishermen three:
>> Wynken,
>> Blynken,
>> And Nod.

EUGENE FIELD

There Was a Knight

There was a knight riding from the east,
Sing the Cather banks, the bonnie broom
Who had been wooing at many a place.
And ye may beguile a young thing soon.

He came unto a widow's door,
Sing the Cather banks, the bonnie broom
And asked where her three daughters were.
And ye may beguile a young thing soon.

"The oldest one's to a washing gone.
Sing the Cather banks, the bonnie broom
The second's to a baking gone.
And ye may beguile a young thing soon.

"The youngest one's to a wedding gone.
Sing the Cather banks, the bonnie broom
And it will be night ere she be home."
And ye may beguile a young thing soon.

He sat him down upon a stone,
Sing the Cather banks, the bonnie broom
Till those three lasses came tripping home.
And ye may beguile a young thing soon.

The oldest one's to the bed making,
Sing the Cather banks, the bonnie broom
And the second one's to the sheet spreading.
And ye may beguile a young thing soon.

The youngest one was bold and bright,
Sing the Cather banks, the bonnie broom
And she was to lie with this unknown knight.
And ye may beguile a young thing soon.

"If ye will answer me questions ten,
Sing the Cather banks, the bonnie broom
The morn ye shall be made my own.
And ye may beguile a young thing soon.

"O what is higher than the tree?
  Sing the Cather banks, the bonnie broom
And what is deeper than the sea?
  And ye may beguile a young thing soon.

"Or what is heavier than the lead?
  Sing the Cather banks, the bonnie broom
And what is better than the bread?
  And ye may beguile a young thing soon.

"O what is whiter than the milk?
  Sing the Cather banks, the bonnie broom
Or what is softer than the silk?
  And ye may beguile a young thing soon.

"Or what is sharper than a thorn?
  Sing the Cather banks, the bonnie broom
Or what is louder than a horn?
  And ye may beguile a young thing soon.

"Or what is greener than the grass?
  Sing the Cather banks, the bonnie broom
Or what is worse than a woman was?"
  And ye may beguile a young thing soon.

"O heaven is higher than the tree.
  Sing the Cather banks, the bonnie broom
And hell is deeper than the sea.
  And ye may beguile a young thing soon.

"O sin is heavier than the lead.
  Sing the Cather banks, the bonnie broom
The blessing's better than the bread.
  And ye may beguile a young thing soon.

"The snow is whiter than the milk,
  Sing the Cather banks, the bonnie broom
And the down is softer than the silk.
  And ye may beguile a young thing soon.

"Hunger is sharper than a thorn,
  Sing the Cather banks, the bonnie broom
And shame is louder than a horn.
  And ye may beguile a young thing soon.

"The pies are greener than the grass,
  Sing the Cather banks, the bonnie broom
And Clootie's worse than a woman was."
  And ye may beguile a young thing soon.

As soon as she the fiend did name,
  Sing the Cather banks, the bonnie broom
He flew away in a blazing flame.
  And ye may beguile a young thing soon.

ANONYMOUS

A Child's Dream

I had a little dog, and my dog was very small;
He licked me in the face, and he answered to my call;
Of all the treasures that were mine, I loved him most of all.

His nose was fresh as morning dew and blacker than the night;
I thought that it could even snuff the shadows and the light;
And his tail he held bravely, like a banner in a fight.

His body covered thick with hair was very good to smell;
His little stomach underneath was pink as any shell;
And I loved him and honored him, more than words can tell.

We ran out in the morning, both of us, to play,
Up and down across the fields for all the sunny day;
But he ran so swiftly—he ran right away.

I looked for him, I called him, entreatingly. Alas,
The dandelions could not speak, though they had seen him pass,
And nowhere was his waving tail among the waving grass.

I called him in a thousand ways and yet he did not come;
The pathways and the hedges were horrible and dumb.
I prayed to God who never heard. My desperate soul grew
    numb.

The sun sank low. I ran; I prayed: "If God has not the power
To find him, let me die. I cannot bear another hour."
When suddenly I came upon a great yellow flower.

And all among its petals, such was Heaven's grace,
In that golden hour, in that golden place,
All among its petals, was his hairy face.

FRANCES CORNFORD

Sandpipers

In the small territory and time
Between one wave and the next, they run
Down the beach and back, eating things
Which seem, conveniently for them,
To surface only when the sand gets wet.
Small, dapper birds, they make me think
Of commuters seen, say, in an early movie
Where the rough screen wavers, where the light
Jerks and seems to rain; of clockwork dolls
Set going on the sidewalk, drawing a crowd
Beside the newsstand at five o'clock; their legs
Black toothpicks, their heads nodding at nothing.
But this comedy is based upon exact
Perceptions, and delicately balanced
Between starvation and the sea:
Though sometimes I have seen one slip and fall,
From either the undertow or greed,
And have to get up in the wave's open mouth,
Still eating, I have never seen
One caught; if necessary he spreads his wings,
With the white stripe, and flutters rather than flies
Out, to begin eating again at once.
Now they are over every outer beach,
Procrastinating steadily southwards
In endlessly local comings and goings.

Whenever a flock of them takes flight,
And flies with the beautiful unison
Of banners in the wind, they are
No longer funny. It is their courage,
Meaningless as the word is when compared
With their thoughtless precisions, which strikes
Between two waves, lost in the sea's
Lost color as they distance me; flying
From winter already, while I

Am in August. When suddenly they turn
In unison, all their bellies shine
Like mirrors flashing white with signals
I cannot read, but I wish them well.

HOWARD NEMEROV

The Dog (As Seen by the Cat)

The Dog is black or white or brown,
  And sometimes spotted like a clown.
He loves to make a foolish noise,
  And Human Company enjoys.

The Human People pat his head
  And teach him to pretend he's dead,
And beg, and fetch, and carry, too;
  Things that no well-bred Cat will do.

At Human jokes, however stale,
  He jumps about and wags his tail,
And Human People clap their hands
  And think he really understands.

They say "Good Dog" to him. To us
  They say "Poor Puss," and make no fuss.
Why Dogs are "good" and Cats are "poor"
  I fail to understand, I'm sure.

To Someone very Good and Just,
  Who has proved worthy of her trust,
A Cat will *sometimes* condescend—
  The Dog is Everybody's friend!

OLIVER HERFORD

The Cowboy's Lament

As I walked out in the streets of Laredo,
As I walked out in Laredo one day,
I spied a poor cowboy wrapped up in white linen,
Wrapped up in white linen as cold as the clay.

"Oh, beat the drum slowly and play the fife lowly,
Play the dead march as you carry me along;
Take me to the green valley, there lay the sod o'er me,
For I'm a young cowboy and I know I've done wrong.

"It was once in the saddle I used to go dashing,
It was once in the saddle I used to go gay;
First to the dram-house and then to the card-house;
Got shot in the breast and I'm dying today.

"Get six jolly cowboys to carry my coffin;
Get six pretty maidens to bear up my pall.
Put bunches of roses all over my coffin,
Put roses to deaden the sods as they fall.

"Then swing your rope slowly and rattle your spurs lowly,
And give a wild whoop as you carry me along;
And in the grave throw me and roll the sod o'er me
For I'm a young cowboy and I know I've done wrong."

We beat the drum slowly and played the fife lowly,
And bitterly wept as we bore him along;
For we all loved our comrade, so brave, young, and handsome,
We all loved our comrade although he'd done wrong.

ANONYMOUS

252

The Midnight Snack

When I was little and he was riled
It never entered my father's head
Not to flare up, roar and turn red.
Mother kept cool and smiled.

Now every night I tiptoe straight
Through my darkened kitchen for
The refrigerator door—
It opens, the inviolate!

Illumined as in dreams I take
A glass of milk, a piece of cake,
Then stealthily retire,

Mindful of how the gas stove's black-
Browed pilot eye's blue fire
Burns into my turned back.

JAMES MERRILL

Casey at the Bat

The outlook wasn't brilliant for the Mudville nine that day;
The score stood four to two with but one inning more to play.
And then when Cooney died at first and Barrows did the same,
A sickly silence fell upon the patrons of the game.

A straggling few got up to go in deep despair. The rest
Clung to the hope which springs eternal in the human breast;
They thought if only Casey could but get a whack at that—
We'd put up even money now with Casey at the bat.

But Flynn preceded Casey, as did also Jimmy Blake,
And the former was a lulu and the latter was a cake;
So upon that stricken multitude grim melancholy sat,
For there seemed but little chance of Casey's getting to the bat.

But Flynn let drive a single, to the wonderment of all,
And Blake, the much despisèd, tore the cover off the ball;
And when the dust had lifted, and the men saw what had
    occurred,
There was Jimmy safe at second and Flynn a-hugging third.

Then from five thousand throats and more there rose a lusty
    yell;
It rumbled through the valley, it rattled in the dell;
It knocked upon the mountain and recoiled upon the flat,
For Casey, mighty Casey, was advancing to the bat.

There was ease in Casey's manner as he stepped into his place;
There was pride in Casey's bearing and a smile on Casey's face.
And when, responding to the cheers, he lightly doffed his hat,
No stranger in the crowd could doubt 'twas Casey at the bat.

Ten thousand eyes were on him as he rubbed his hands with
    dirt;
Five thousand tongues applauded when he wiped them on his
    shirt.
Then while the writhing pitcher ground the ball into his hip,
Defiance gleamed in Casey's eye, a sneer curled Casey's lip.

And now the leather-covered sphere came hurtling through the
    air,
And Casey stood a-watching it in haughty grandeur there.
Close by the sturdy batsman the ball unheeded sped—
"That ain't my style," said Casey. "Strike one," the umpire said.

From the benches, black with people, there went up a muffled
    roar,
Like the beating of the storm waves on a stern and distant
    shore.
"Kill him! Kill the umpire!" shouted someone on the stand;
And it's likely they'd have killed him had not Casey raised his
    hand.

With a smile of Christian charity great Casey's visage shone;
He stilled the rising tumult; he bade the game go on;
He signaled to the pitcher, and once more the spheroid flew;
But Casey still ignored it, and the umpire said, "Strike two."

"Fraud!" cried the maddened thousands, and echo answered,
    "Fraud!"
But one scornful look from Casey and the audience was awed.
They saw his face grow stern and cold, they saw his muscles
    strain,
And they knew that Casey wouldn't let that ball go by again.

The sneer is gone from Casey's lip, his teeth are clenched in
    hate;
He pounds with cruel violence his bat upon the plate.
And now the pitcher holds the ball, and now he lets it go,
And now the air is shattered by the force of Casey's blow.

Oh, somewhere in this favored land the sun is shining bright;
The band is playing somewhere, and somewhere hearts are light,
And somewhere men are laughing, and somewhere children
    shout;
But there is no joy in Mudville—mighty Casey has struck out.

ERNEST LAWRENCE THAYER

The Bat

By day the bat is cousin to the mouse.
He likes the attic of an ageing house.

His fingers make a hat about his head.
His pulse beat is so slow we think him dead.

He loops in crazy figures half the night
Among the trees that face the corner light.

But when he brushes up against a screen,
We are afraid of what our eyes have seen:

For something is amiss or out of place
When mice with wings can wear a human face.

THEODORE ROETHKE

A Poison Tree

I was angry with my friend:
I told my wrath, my wrath did end.
I was angry with my foe:
I told it not, my wrath did grow.

And I waterd it in fears,
Night & morning with my tears;
And I sunnéd it with smiles,
And with soft deceitful wiles.

And it grew both day and night,
Till it bore an apple bright.
And my foe beheld it shine,
And he knew that it was mine,

And into my garden stole,
When the night had veild the pole;
In the morning glad I see
My foe outstretchd beneath the tree.

WILLIAM BLAKE

There is no Frigate like a Book
To take us Lands away
Nor any Coursers like a Page
Of prancing Poetry—
This Travel may the poorest take
Without offence of Toll—
How frugal is the Chariot
That bears the Human soul.

EMILY DICKINSON

A Circus Garland

PARADE

This is the day the circus comes
With blare of brass, with beating drums,
And clashing cymbals, and with roar
Of wild beasts never heard before
Within town limits. Spick and span
Will shine each gilded cage and van;
Cockades at every horse's head
Will nod, and riders dressed in red
Or blue trot by. There will be floats
In shapes like dragons, thrones and boats,
And clowns on stilts; freaks big and small,
Till leisurely and last of all
Camels and elephants will pass
Beneath our elms, along our grass.

THE PERFORMING SEAL

Who is so proud
As not to feel
A secret awe
Before a seal
That keeps such sleek
And wet repose
While twirling candles
On his nose?

GUNGA

With wrinkled hide and great frayed ears,
Gunga, the elephant, appears.
Colored like city smoke he goes
As gingerly on blunted toes
As if he held the earth in trust
And feared to hurt the very dust.

259

EQUESTRIENNE

See, they are clearing the sawdust course
For the girl in pink on the milk-white horse.
Her spangles twinkle; his pale flanks shine,
Every hair of his tail is fine
And bright as a comet's; his mane blows free,
And she points a toe and bends a knee,
And while his hoofbeats fall like rain
Over and over and over again.
And nothing that moves on land or sea
Will seem so beautiful to me
As the girl in pink on the milk-white horse
Cantering over the sawdust course.

EPILOGUE

Nothing now to mark the spot
But a littered vacant lot;
Sawdust in a heap, and there
Where the ring was, grass worn bare
In a circle, scuffed and brown,
And a paper hoop the clown
Made his little dog jump through,
And a pygmy pony-shoe.

RACHEL FIELD

By Frazier Creek Falls

Standing up on lifted, folded rock
looking out and down—

The creek falls to a far valley.
hills beyond that
facing, half-forested, dry
—clear sky
strong wind in the
stiff glittering needle clusters
of the pine—their brown
round trunk bodies
straight, still;
rustling trembling limbs and twigs

listen.

This living flowing land
is all there is, forever

We *are* it
it sings through us—

We could live on this Earth
without clothes or tools!

GARY SNYDER

Ozymandias

I met a traveler from an antique land
Who said: Two vast and trunkless legs of stone
Stand in the desert . . . Near them, on the sand,
Half sunk, a shattered visage lies, whose frown,
And wrinkled lip, and sneer of cold command,
Tell that its sculptor well those passions read
Which yet survive, stamped on these lifeless things,
The hand that mocked them, and the heart that fed:
And on the pedestal these words appear:
"My name is Ozymandias, king of kings:
Look on my works, ye Mighty, and despair!"
Nothing beside remains. Round the decay
Of that colossal wreck, boundless and bare
The lone and level sands stretch far away.

PERCY BYSSHE SHELLEY

The Caterpillar

Brown and furry
Caterpillar in a hurry
Take your walk
To the shady leaf or stalk
Or what not,
Which may be the chosen spot.
No toad spy you,
Hovering bird of prey pass by you;
Spin and die,
To live again a butterfly.

CHRISTINA ROSSETTI

I'm Nobody! Who are you?
Are you—Nobody—too?
Then there's a pair of us!
Dont tell! they'd banish us—you know!

How dreary—to be—Somebody!
How public—like a Frog—
To tell your name—the livelong June—
To an admiring Bog!

EMILY DICKINSON

Dandelion

These lions, each by a daisy queen,
With yellow manes, and golden mien,
Keep so still for wind to start
They stare, like eyes that have no smart.
But, once they hear that shepherd pipe,
Down meadows and through orchards ripe,
They dance together, lion and daisy,
Through long midday, slow and lazy;
Each dandelion in his fierce lust
Forgets the sunset's reddy rust;
Now by night winds roughly kissed
His mane becomes a clock of mist
Which mortal breath next morn will blow,
While his white virgins bloom below.

SACHEVERELL SITWELL

On the Grasshopper and Cricket

The poetry of earth is never dead:
  When all the birds are faint with the hot sun,
  And hide in cooling trees, a voice will run
From hedge to hedge about the new-mown mead—
That is the Grasshopper's. He takes the lead
  In summer luxury; he has never done
  With his delights, for when tired out with fun
He rests at ease beneath some pleasant weed.
The poetry of earth is ceasing never:
  On a lone winter evening, when the frost
    Has wrought a silence, from the stove there shrills
The Cricket's song, in warmth increasing ever,
  And seems to one in drowsiness half lost,
    The Grasshopper's among some grassy hills.

JOHN KEATS

Gracious Goodness

On the beach where we had been idly
telling the shell coins
cat's paw, cross-barred Venus, china cockle,
we both saw at once
the sea bird fall to the sand
and flap grotesquely.
He had taken a great barbed hook
out through the cheek and fixed
in the big wing.
He was pinned to himself to die,
a royal tern with a black crest blown back
as if he flew in his own private wind.
He felt good in my hands, not fragile
but muscular and glossy and strong,
the beak that could have split my hand
opening only to cry
as we yanked on the barbs.
We borrowed a clippers, cut and drew out the hook.
Then the royal tern took off, wavering,
lurched twice,
then acrobat returned to his element, dipped,
zoomed, and sailed out to dive for a fish.
Virtue: what a sunrise in the belly.
Why is there nothing
I have ever done with anybody
that seems to me so obviously right?

MARGE PIERCY

The Babes in the Wood

My dear, do you know,
How a long time ago,
 Two poor little children,
Whose names I don't know,
Were stolen away
On a fine summer's day,
 And left in a wood,
As I've heard people say.

Among the trees high
Beneath the blue sky
 They plucked the bright flowers
And watched the birds fly;
Then on blackberries fed,
And strawberries red,
 And when they were weary
"We'll go home," they said.

And when it was night
So sad was their plight,
 The sun it went down,
And the moon gave no light.
They sobbed and they sighed
And they bitterly cried,
 And long before morning
They lay down and died.

And when they were dead,
The robins so red
 Brought strawberry leaves
And over them spread;
And all the day long,
The green branches among,
 They'd prettily whistle
And this was their song—
"Poor babes in the wood!

Sweet babes in the wood!
Oh the sad fate of
The babes in the wood!"

ANONYMOUS

Song of the Queen Bee

*"The breeding of the bee," says a United States
Department of Agriculture bulletin on artificial
insemination, "has always been handicapped by
the fact that the queen mates in the air with whatever drone she encounters."*

When the air is wine and the wind is free
And the morning sits on the lovely lea
And sunlight ripples on every tree,
Then love-in-air is the thing for me—
 I'm a bee,
 I'm a ravishing, rollicking, young queen bee,
 That's me.

I wish to state that I think it's great,
Oh, it's simply rare in the upper air,
 It's the place to pair
 With a bee.
Let old geneticists plot and plan,
They're stuffy people, to a man;
Let gossips whisper behind their fan.
 (Oh, she *does?*
 Buzz, buzz, buzz!)
My nuptial flight is sheer delight;
I'm a giddy girl who likes to swirl,
 To fly and soar
 And fly some more,
  I'm a bee.
And I wish to state that I'll *always* mate
 With whatever drone I encounter.

There's a kind of a wild and glad elation
In the natural way of insemination;
Who thinks that love is a handicap
Is a fuddydud and a common sap,
For I am a queen and I am a bee,

270

I'm devil-may-care and I'm fancy-free,
The test tube doesn't appeal to me,
  Not me,
  I'm a bee.
And I'm here to state that I'll *always* mate
  With whatever drone I encounter.

Let mares and cows, by calculating,
Improve themselves with loveless mating,
Let groundlings breed in the modern fashion,
I'll stick to the air and the grand old passion;
I may be small and I'm just a bee
But I *won't* have Science improving *me*,
  Not me,
  I'm a bee.
On a day that's fair with a wind that's free,
Any old drone is the lad for me.

I have no flair for love *moderne*,
It's far too studied, far too stern,
I'm just a bee—I'm wild, I'm free,
  That's me.
I can't afford to be too choosy;
In every queen there's a touch of floozy,
  And it's simply rare
  In the upper air
  And I wish to state
  That I'll *always* mate
With whatever drone I encounter.

Man is a fool for the latest movement,
He broods and broods on race improvement;
What boots it to improve a bee
If it means the end of ecstasy?
  (He ought to be there
  On a day that's fair,
  Oh, it's simply rare
    For a bee.)

Man's so wise he is growing foolish,
Some of his schemes are downright ghoulish;
He owns a bomb that'll end creation
And he wants to change the sex relation,
He thinks that love is a handicap,
He's a fuddydud, he's a simple sap;
Man is a meddler, man's a boob,
He looks for love in the depths of a tube,
His restless mind is forever ranging,
He thinks he's advancing as long as he's changing,
He cracks the atom, he racks his skull,
Man is meddlesome, man is dull,
Man is busy instead of idle,
Man is alarmingly suicidal,
   Me, I'm a bee.

I am a bee and I simply love it,
I am a bee and I'm darned glad of it,
I am a bee, I know about love:
You go upstairs, you go above,
You do not pause to dine or sup,
The sky won't wait—it's a long trip up;
You rise, you soar, you take the blue,
It's you and me, kid, me and you,
It's everything, it's the nearest drone,
It's never a thing that you find alone.
   I'm a bee,
   I'm free.

If any old farmer can keep and hive me,
Then any old drone may catch and wive me;
I'm sorry for creatures who cannot pair
On a gorgeous day in the upper air,
I'm sorry for cows who have to boast
Of affairs they've had by parcel post,
I'm sorry for man with his plots and guile,
His test-tube manner, his test-tube smile;
I'll multiply and I'll increase

As I always have—by mere caprice;
For I am a queen and I am a bee,
I'm devil-may-care and I'm fancy-free,
Love-in-air is the thing for me,
   Oh, it's simply *rare*
   In the beautiful air,
     And I wish to state
     That I'll *always* mate
With whatever drone I encounter.

E. B. WHITE

Infant Sorrow

My mother groand! my father wept.
Into the dangerous world I leapt:
Helpless, naked, piping loud:
Like a fiend hid in a cloud.

Struggling in my father's hands,
Striving against my swadling bands,
Bound and weary I thought best
To sulk upon my mother's breast.

WILLIAM BLAKE

The Solitary Reaper

Behold her, single in the field,
Yon solitary Highland Lass!
Reaping and singing by herself;
Stop here, or gently pass!
Alone she cuts and binds the grain,
And sings a melancholy strain;
O listen! for the Vale profound
Is overflowing with the sound.

No Nightingale did ever chaunt
More welcome notes to weary bands
Of travellers in some shady haunt,
Among Arabian sands;
A voice so thrilling ne'er was heard
In springtime from the Cuckoo bird.
Breaking the silence of the seas
Among the farthest Hebrides.

Will no one tell me what she sings?
Perhaps the plaintive numbers flow
For old, unhappy, far-off things,
And battles long ago;
Or is it some more humble lay,
Familiar matter of today?
Some natural sorrow, loss, or pain,
That has been, and may be again?

Whate'er the theme, the Maiden sang
As if her song could have no ending;
I saw her singing at her work,
And o'er the sickle bending;—
I listened, motionless and still;
And, as I mounted up the hill,
The music in my heart I bore
Long after it was heard no more.

WILLIAM WORDSWORTH

South

Today's cool asphalt . . . where had the cars gone,
I asked myself a few miles farther on?
I thumbed the few that passed me but none slowed,
Even a farm-truck creaking with its load
—And glimpsed through glass a dusty slash of laugh
Before the bulk laboriously turned off
Toward distant barns. All I could see both ways
Was road now, straightness wobbling in the haze
Heat hatched between the poplars. Southward, true,
But the real traffic must be moving through
On some bypass. I stepped on, obstinate,
Somehow unwilling to turn back on it,
This unrewarding road, as if I liked
Its very hardness, till by noon I'd hiked
To where it slightly bent at a dry oak
Upon a rising, thinly grassed, that broke
The double line of poplars on one side.
Here where the chips of acorn-cups had dried,
Where there was weak shade, though without a breeze,
I sat down firmly to my bread and cheese.

My back-pack, as familiar as my name,
Stood there beside me in its large light frame,
And as I munched I came to realize
That I was not encumbered otherwise
By furniture or promises because
Carrying my needs I carried all I was,
A gust on asphalt between origin
And destinations. That was it! I'd been,
Unawares all my life, the transient
Of that "between" through which I went and went
But never thought of other than as way
To somewhere else. Yet sitting here today
On meager grass walled-in with insect sound,
I thought I rested on sufficient ground.

Mouth full, I found myself abruptly free
From all anxiety. I would reach, maybe,
The South in my own time, maybe would not.
Meanwhile cut loose yet wholly here, parched, hot,
On the wrong road, I started off again
But did not look back every now and then
Expecting rides, and it was not the same.

At the end of a long afternoon I came
To some youth hostel on the official list
Which by that morning's plan I would have missed:
The only other occupant and I
Shared wine; trees I could not identify
Reared in green blossom near a wide stone well;
My night was haunted by their agile smell.

THOM GUNN

The Splendor Falls

The splendor falls on castle walls
  And snowy summits old in story;
The long light shakes across the lakes,
  And the wild cataract leaps in glory.
Blow, bugle, blow, set the wild echoes flying,
Blow, bugle; answer, echoes, dying, dying, dying.

O, hark, O, hear! how thin and clear,
  And thinner, clearer, farther going!
O, sweet and far from cliff and scar
  The horns of Elfland faintly blowing!
Blow, let us hear the purple glens replying,
Blow, bugle; answer, echoes, dying, dying, dying.

O love, they die in yon rich sky,
  They faint on hill or field or river;
Our echoes roll from soul to soul,
  And grow forever and forever.
Blow, bugle, blow, set the wild echoes flying,
And answer, echoes, answer, dying, dying, dying.

ALFRED, LORD TENNYSON

The Fairies

Up the airy mountain,
  Down the rushy glen.
We daren't go a-hunting
  For fear of little men;
Wee folk, good folk,
  Trooping all together;
Green jacket, red cap,
  And white owl's feather!

Down along the rocky shore
  Some make their home.
They live on crispy pancakes
  Of yellow tide-foam;
Some in the reeds
  Of the black mountain-lake,
With frogs for their watch-dogs,
  All night awake.

High on the hill-top
  The old King sits;
He is now so old and gray
  He's nigh lost his wits.
With a bridge of white mist
  Columbkill he crosses,
On his stately journeys
  From Slieveleague to Rosses;
Or going up with music
  On cold starry nights,
To sup with the Queen
  Of the gay Northern Lights.

They stole little Bridget
  For seven years long;
When she came down again
  Her friends were all gone.
They took her lightly back,

Between the night and morrow,
They thought that she was fast asleep,
But she was dead with sorrow.
They have kept her ever since
Deep within the lake,
On a bed of flag-leaves,
Watching till she wake.

By the craggy hill-side,
Through the mosses bare,
They have planted thorn-trees
For pleasure here and there.
Is any man so daring
As to dig one up in spite,
He shall find the thornies set
In his bed at night.

Up the airy mountain,
Down the rushy glen,
We daren't go a-hunting
For fear of little men;
Wee folk, good folk,
Trooping all together;
Green jacket, red cap,
And white owl's feather!

WILLIAM ALLINGHAM

La Belle Dame sans Merci

"O what can ail thee, Knight at arms,
  Alone and palely loitering?
The sedge has withered from the Lake
  And no birds sing!

"O what can ail thee, Knight at arms,
  So haggard, and so woebegone?
"The squirrel's granary is full
  And the harvest's done.

"I see a lily on thy brow
  With anguish moist and fever dew,
And on thy cheeks a fading rose
  Fast withereth too."

"I met a Lady in the Meads,
  Full beautiful, a faery's child,
Her hair was long, her foot was light
  And her eyes were wild.

"I made a Garland for her head,
  And bracelets too, and fragrant Zone;
She looked at me as she did love
  And made sweet moan.

"I set her on my pacing steed
  And nothing else saw all day long,
For sidelong would she bend and sing
  A faery's song.

"She found me roots of relish sweet,
  And honey wild, and manna dew,
And sure in language strange she said
  'I love thee true.'

"She took me to her elfin grot
  And there she wept and sighed full sore,
And there I shut her wild wild eyes
  With kisses four.

"And there she lullèd me asleep,
  And there I dreamed, Ah Woe betide!
The latest dream I ever dreamt
  On the cold hill side.

"I saw pale Kings, and Princes too,
  Pale warriors, death-pale were they all;
They cried, 'La belle dame sans merci
  Thee hath in thrall!'

"I saw their starved lips in the gloam
  With horrid warning gapèd wide,
And I awoke, and found me here
  On the cold hill's side.

"And this is why I sojourn here,
  Alone and palely loitering;
Though the sedge is withered from the Lake
  And no birds sing."

JOHN KEATS

The Land of Nod

From breakfast on through all the day
At home among my friends I stay,
But every night I go abroad
Afar into the Land of Nod.

All by myself I have to go,
With none to tell me what to do—
All alone beside the streams
And up the mountain-sides of dreams.

The strangest things are there for me,
Both things to eat and things to see,
And many frightening sights abroad
Till morning in the Land of Nod.

Try as I like to find the way,
I never can get back by day,
Nor can remember plain and clear
The curious music that I hear.

ROBERT LOUIS STEVENSON

A Boy's Song

Where the pools are bright and deep,
Where the gray trout lies asleep,
Up the river and o'er the lea,
That's the way for Billy and me.

Where the blackbird sings the latest,
Where the hawthorn blooms the sweetest,
Where the nestlings chirp and flee,
That's the way for Billy and me.

Where the mowers mow the cleanest,
Where the hay lies thick and greenest,
There to trace the homeward bee,
That's the way for Billy and me.

Where the hazel bank is steepest,
Where the shadow falls the deepest,
Where the clustering nuts fall free,
That's the way for Billy and me.

Why the boys should drive away
Little sweet maidens from their play,
Or love to banter and fight so well,
That's the thing I never could tell.

But this I know, I love to play,
Through the meadow, among the hay;
Up the water and o'er the lea,
That's the way for Billy and me.

JAMES HOGG

Fear No More the Heat o' the Sun

Fear no more the heat o' the sun,
　　Nor the furious winter's rages;
Thou thy worldly task hast done,
　　Home art gone, and ta'en thy wages:
Golden lads and girls all must,
As chimney-sweepers, come to dust.

Fear no more the frown o' the great;
　　Thou art past the tyrant's stroke;
Care no more to clothe and eat;
　　To thee the reed is as the oak:
The scepter, learning, physic, must
All follow this, and come to dust.

Fear no more the lightning flash,
　　Nor the all-dreaded thunder stone;
Fear not slander, censure rash;
　　Thou hast finished joy and moan:
All lovers young, all lovers must
Consign to thee, and come to dust.

No exorciser harm thee!
Nor no witchcraft charm thee!
Ghost unlaid forbear thee!
Nothing ill come near thee!
Quiet consummation have;
And renownéd be thy grave!

WILLIAM SHAKESPEARE

Under the Waterfall

"Whenever I plunge my arm, like this,
In a basin of water, I never miss
The sweet sharp sense of a fugitive day
Fetched back from its thickening shroud of gray.
  Hence the only prime
  And real love-rhyme
  That I know by heart,
  And that leaves no smart,
Is the purl of a little valley fall
About three spans wide and two spans tall
Over a table of solid rock,
And into a scoop of the self-same block;
The purl of a runlet that never ceases
In stir of kingdoms, in wars, in peaces;
With a hollow boiling voice it speaks
And has spoken since hills were turfless peaks."

"And why gives this the only prime
Idea to you of a real love-rhyme?
And why does plunging your arm in a bowl
Full of spring water, bring throbs to your soul?"

"Well, under the fall, in a crease of the stone,
Though where precisely none ever has known,
Jammed darkly, nothing to show how prized,
And by now with its smoothness opalized,
  Is a drinking-glass:
  For, down that pass
  My lover and I
  Walked under a sky
Of blue with a leaf-wove awning of green,
In the burn of August, to paint the scene,
And we placed our basket of fruit and wine
By the runlet's rim, where we sat to dine;
And when we had drunk from the glass together,

Arched by the oak-copse from the weather,
I held the vessel to rinse in the fall,
Where it slipped, and sank, and was past recall,
Though we stooped and plumbed the little abyss
With long bared arms. There the glass still is.
And, as said, if I thrust my arm below
Cold water in basin or bowl, a throe
From the past awakens a sense of that time,
And the glass we used, and the cascade's rhyme.
The basin seems the pool, and its edge
The hard smooth face of the brook-side ledge,
And the leafy pattern of china-ware
The hanging plants that were bathing there.

"By night, by day, when it shines or lours,
There lies intact that chalice of ours,
And its presence adds to the rhyme of love
Persistently sung by the fall above.
No lip has touched it since his and mine
In turns therefrom sipped lovers' wine."

THOMAS HARDY

A Glass of Beer

The lanky hank of a she in the inn over there
Nearly killed me for asking the loan of a glass of beer;
May the devil grip the whey-faced slut by the hair,
And beat bad manners out of her skin for a year.

That parboiled ape, with the toughest jaw you will see
On virtue's path, and a voice that would rasp the dead,
Came roaring and raging the minute she looked at me,
And threw me out of the house on the back of my head!

If I asked her master he'd give me a cask a day;
But she, with the beer at hand, not a gill would arrange!
May she marry a ghost and bear him a kitten, and may
The High King of Glory permit her to get the mange.

JAMES STEPHENS

We Real Cool

                    The Pool Players.
                Seven at the Golden Shovel.

We real cool. We
Left school. We

Lurk late. We
Strike straight. We

Sing sin. We
Thin gin. We

Jazz June. We
Die soon.

                    GWENDOLYN BROOKS

But He Was Cool
or: He Even Stopped for Green Lights

super-cool
ultrablack
a tan/purple
had a beautiful shade.

he had a double-natural
that wd put the sisters to shame.
his dashikis were tailor made
& his beads were imported sea shells
    (from some blk/country i never heard of)
he was triple-hip.

his tikis were hand carved
out of ivory
& came express from the motherland.
he would greet u in swahili
& say good-by in yoruba.
woooooooooooo-jim he bes so cool & ill tel li gent
        cool-cool is so cool he was un-cooled by other nig-
           gers' cool
        cool-cool ultracool was bop-cool/ice box cool so cool
           cold cool
        his wine didn't have to be cooled, him was air condi-
           tioned cool
        cool-cool/real cool made me cool—now ain't that
           cool
        cool-cool so cool him nick-named refrigerator.

cool-cool so cool
he didn't know,
after detroit, newark, chicago &c.,
we had to hip
    cool-cool/ super-cool/ real cool
  that
to be black
is
to be
very-hot.

       DON L. LEE

The Instruction Manual

As I sit looking out of a window of the building
I wish I did not have to write the instruction manual on the uses
    of a new metal.
I look down into the street and see people, each walking with an
    inner peace,
And envy them—they are so far away from me!
Not one of them has to worry about getting out this manual on
    schedule.
And, as my way is, I begin to dream, resting my elbows on the desk
    and leaning out of the window a little,
Of dim Guadalajara! City of rose-colored flowers!
City I wanted most to see, and most did not see, in Mexico!
But I fancy I see, under the press of having to write the instruction
    manual,
Your public square, city, with its elaborate little bandstand!
The band is playing *Scheherazade* by Rimsky-Korsakov.
Around stand the flower girls, handing out rose- and lemon-colored
    flowers,
Each attractive in her rose-and-blue striped dress (Oh! such shades
    of rose and blue),
And nearby is the little white booth where women in green serve
    you green and yellow fruit.
The couples are parading; everyone is in a holiday mood.
First, leading the parade, is a dapper fellow
Clothed in deep blue. On his head sits a white hat
And he wears a mustache, which has been trimmed for the occasion.
His dear one, his wife, is young and pretty; her shawl is rose, pink,
    and white.
Her slippers are patent leather, in the American fashion,
And she carries a fan, for she is modest, and does not want the crowd
    to see her face too often.
But everybody is so busy with his wife or loved one
I doubt they would notice the mustachioed man's wife.
Here come the boys! They are skipping and throwing little things

on the sidewalk

Which is made of gray tile. One of them, a little older, has a toothpick in his teeth.

He is silenter than the rest, and affects not to notice the pretty young girls in white.

But his friends notice them, and shout their jeers at the laughing girls.

Yet soon all this will cease, with the deepening of their years,

And love bring each to the parade grounds for another reason.

But I have lost sight of the young fellow with the toothpick.

Wait—there he is—on the other side of the bandstand,

Secluded from his friends, in earnest talk with a young girl

Of fourteen or fifteen. I try to hear what they are saying

But it seems they are just mumbling something—shy words of love, probably.

She is slightly taller than he, and looks quietly down into his sincere eyes.

She is wearing white. The breeze ruffles her long fine black hair against her olive cheek.

Obviously she is in love. The boy, the young boy with the toothpick, he is in love too;

His eyes show it. Turning from this couple,

I see there is an intermission in the concert.

The paraders are resting and sipping drinks through straws

(The drinks are dispensed from a large glass crock by a lady in dark blue),

And the musicians mingle among them, in their creamy white uniforms, and talk

About the weather, perhaps, or how their kids are doing at school.

Let us take this opportunity to tiptoe into one of the side streets.

Here you may see one of those white houses with green trim

That are so popular here. Look—I told you!

It is cool and dim inside, but the patio is sunny.

An old woman in gray sits there, fanning herself with a palm leaf fan.

She welcomes us to her patio, and offers us a cooling drink.

"My son is in Mexico City," she says. "He would welcome you too

If he were here. But his job is with a bank there.
Look, here is a photograph of him."
And a dark-skinned lad with pearly teeth grins out at us from the
worn leather frame.
We thank her for her hospitality, for it is getting late
And we must catch a view of the city, before we leave, from a good
high place.
That church tower will do—the faded pink one, there against the
fierce blue of the sky. Slowly we enter.
The caretaker, an old man dressed in brown and gray, asks us how
long we have been in the city, and how we like it here.
His daughter is scrubbing the steps—she nods to us as we pass into
the tower.
Soon we have reached the top, and the whole network of the city
extends before us.
There is the rich quarter, with its houses of pink and white, and its
crumbling, leafy terraces.
There is the poorer quarter, its homes a deep blue.
There is the market, where men are selling hats and swatting flies
And there is the public library, painted several shades of pale green
and beige.
Look! There is the square we just came from, with the promenad-
ers.
There are fewer of them, now that the heat of the day has increased,
But the young boy and girl still lurk in the shadows of the band-
stand.
And there is the home of the little old lady—
She is still sitting in the patio, fanning herself.
How limited, but how complete withal, has been our experience of
Guadalajara!
We have seen young love, married love, and the love of an aged
mother for her son.
We have heard the music, tasted the drinks, and looked at colored
houses.

What more is there to do, except stay? And that we cannot do.
And as a last breeze freshens the top of the weathered old tower,
    I turn my gaze
Back to the instruction manual which has made me dream of Guada-
    lajara.

JOHN ASHBERY

Poor Old Lady

Poor old lady, she swallowed a fly.
I don't know why she swallowed a fly.
Poor old lady, I think she'll die.

Poor old lady, she swallowed a spider.
It squirmed and wriggled and turned inside her.
She swallowed the spider to catch the fly.
I don't know why she swallowed a fly.
Poor old lady, I think she'll die.

Poor old lady, she swallowed a bird.
How absurd! She swallowed a bird.
She swallowed the bird to catch the spider,
She swallowed the spider to catch the fly,
I don't know why she swallowed a fly.
Poor old lady, I think she'll die.

Poor old lady, she swallowed a cat.
Think of that! She swallowed a cat.
She swallowed the cat to catch the bird.
She swallowed the bird to catch the spider.
She swallowed the spider to catch the fly,
I don't know why she swallowed a fly.
Poor old lady, I think she'll die.

Poor old lady, she swallowed a dog.
She went the whole hog when she swallowed the dog.
She swallowed the dog to catch the cat,
She swallowed the cat to catch the bird,
She swallowed the bird to catch the spider.
She swallowed the spider to catch the fly,
I don't know why she swallowed a fly.
Poor old lady, I think she'll die.

Poor old lady, she swallowed a cow.
I don't know how she swallowed the cow.
She swallowed the cow to catch the dog,

She swallowed the dog to catch the cat,
She swallowed the cat to catch the bird,
She swallowed the bird to catch the spider,
She swallowed the spider to catch the fly,
I don't know why she swallowed a fly.
Poor old lady, I think she'll die.

Poor old lady, she swallowed a horse.
She died, of course.

ANONYMOUS

A narrow Fellow in the Grass
Occasionally rides—
You may have met Him—did you not
His notice sudden is—

The Grass divides as with a Comb—
A spotted shaft is seen—
And then it closes at your feet
And opens further on—

He likes a Boggy Acre
A Floor too cool for Corn—
Yet when a Boy, and Barefoot—
I more than once at Noon
Have passed, I thought, a Whip lash
Unbraiding in the Sun
When stooping to secure it
It wrinkled, and was gone—

Several of Nature's People
I know, and they know me—
I feel for them a transport
Of cordiality—

But never met this Fellow
Attended, or alone
Without a tighter breathing
And Zero at the Bone—

EMILY DICKINSON

Say Not the Struggle Nought Availeth

Say not the struggle nought availeth,
    The labor and the wounds are vain,
The enemy faints not, nor faileth,
    And as things have been they remain.

If hopes were dupes, fears may be liars;
    It may be, in yon smoke concealed,
Your comrades chase e'en now the fliers,
    And, but for you, possess the field.

For while the tired waves, vainly breaking,
    Seem here no painful inch to gain,
Far back, through creeks and inlets making,
    Comes silent, flooding in, the main.

And not by eastern windows only,
    When daylight comes, comes in the light,
In front, the sun climbs slow, how slowly,
    But westward, look, the land is bright.

                              ARTHUR HUGH CLOUGH

The Night Piece, to Julia

Her eyes the glowworm lend thee;
The shooting stars attend thee;
   And the elves also,
   Whose little eyes glow
Like the sparks of fire, befriend thee.

No will-o'-the-wisp mislight thee;
Nor snake or slowworm bite thee;
   But on, on thy way,
   Not making a stay,
Since ghost there's none to affright thee.

Let not the dark thee cumber;
What though the moon does slumber?
   The stars of the night
   Will lend thee their light,
Like tapers clear without number.

Then, Julia, let me woo thee,
Thus, thus to come unto me;
   And when I shall meet
   Thy silvery feet,
My soul I'll pour into thee.

ROBERT HERRICK

The Twa Brothers

There were twa brethren in the north,
  They went to the school thegither;
The one unto the other said,
  Will you try a warsle, brither?

They warsled up, they warsled down,
  Till Sir John fell to the ground;
And there was a knife in Sir Willie's pouch
  Gied him a deadlie wound.

Oh brither dear, take me on your back,
  Carry me to yon burn clear;
And wash the blood from off my wound
  And it will bleed nae mair.

He took him up upon his back,
  Carried him to yon burn clear
And wash'd the blood from off his wound,
  But aye it bled the mair.

Oh brither dear, take me on your back,
  Carry me to yon kirk-yard,
And dig a grave baith wide and deep
  And lay my body there.

He's ta'en him up upon his back,
  Carried him to yon kirk-yard,
And dug a grave baith deep and wide
  And laid his body there.

But what will I say to my father dear,
  Gin he chance to say, Willie, whar's John?
Oh say that he's to England gone
  To buy him a cask of wine.

And what will I say to my mother dear,
  Gin she chance to say, Willie, whar's John?
Oh say that he's to England gone
  To buy her a new silk gown.

And what will I say to my sister dear,
   Gin she chance to say, Willie, whar's John?
Oh say that he 's to England gone
   To buy her a wedding ring.

But what will I say to her you lo'e dear,
   Gin she cry, Why tarries my John?
Oh tell her I lie in Kirk-land fair,
   And home again will never come.

ANONYMOUS

The Fallow Deer at the Lonely House

One without looks in to-night
   Through the curtain-chink
From the sheet of glistening white;
One without looks in to-night
   As we sit and think
   By the fender-brink.

We do not discern those eyes
   Watching in the snow;
Lit by lamps of rosy dyes
We do not discern those eyes
   Wondering, aglow,
   Fourfooted, tiptoe.

THOMAS HARDY

The Song of Wandering Aengus

I went out to the hazel wood,
Because a fire was in my head,
And cut and peeled a hazel wand,
And hooked a berry to a thread;
And when white moths were on the wing,
And moth-like stars were flickering out,
I dropped the berry in a stream
And caught a little silver trout.

When I had laid it on the floor
I went to blow the fire aflame,
But something rustled on the floor,
And some one called me by my name:
It had become a glimmering girl
With apple blossom in her hair
Who called me by my name and ran
And faded through the brightening air.

Though I am old with wandering
Through hollow lands and hilly lands,
I will find out where she has gone,
And kiss her lips and take her hands;
And walk among long dappled grass,
And pluck till time and times are done
The silver apples of the moon,
The golden apples of the sun.

WILLIAM BUTLER YEATS

World

Breakers at high tide shoot
spray over the jetty boulders
that collects in shallow chips, depressions,

evening the surface to run-off level:
of these possible worlds of held water,
most can't outlast the interim tideless

drought, so are clear, sterile, encased with
salt: one in particular, though, a hole,
providing depth with little surface,

keeps water through the hottest day:
a slime of green algae extends into that
tiny sea, and animals tiny enough to be in a

world there breed and dart and breathe and
die: so we are here in this plant-created oxygen,
drinking this sweet rain, consuming this green.

A. R. AMMONS

The Rime of the Ancient Mariner

in Seven Parts

Argument

How a Ship, having first sailed to the Equator, was driven by storms to the cold Country towards the South Pole; how the Ancient Mariner cruelly and in contempt of the laws of hospitality killed a Sea-bird and how he was followed by many and strange Judgments: and in what manner he came back to his own Country.

Part I

An ancient Mariner meeteth three Gallants bidden to a wedding feast, and detaineth one.

It is an ancient Mariner
And he stoppeth one of three.
—"By thy long gray beard and glittering eye,
Now wherefore stopp'st thou me?

The Bridegroom's doors are opened wide,
And I am next of kin;
The guests are met, the feast is set:
May'st hear the merry din."

He holds him with his skinny hand,
"There was a ship," quoth he.
"Hold off! unhand me, graybeard loon!"
Eftsoons his hand dropped he.

The Wedding Guest is spellbound by the eye of the old seafaring man, and constrained to hear his tale.

He holds him with his glittering eye—
The Wedding Guest stood still,
And listens like a three years' child:
The Mariner hath his will.

The Wedding Guest sat on a stone:
He cannot choose but hear;
And thus spake on that ancient man,
The bright-eyed Mariner.

"The ship was cheered, the harbor cleared,
Merrily did we drop
Below the kirk, below the hill,
Below the lighthouse top.

The Mariner
tells how the ship
sailed southward
with a good wind
and fair weather,
till it reached the
line.

The Sun came up upon the left,
Out of the sea came he!
And he shone bright, and on the right
Went down into the sea.

Higher and higher every day,
Till over the mast at noon—"
The Wedding Guest here beat his breast,
For he heard the loud bassoon.

The Wedding
Guest heareth the
bridal music; but
the Mariner
continueth his
tale.

The bride hath paced into the hall,
Red as a rose is she;
Nodding their heads before her goes
The merry minstrelsy.

The Wedding Guest he beat his breast,
Yet he cannot choose but hear;
And thus spake on that ancient man,
The bright-eyed Mariner.

The ship driven
by a storm
toward the South
Pole.

"And now the STORM-BLAST came, and he
Was tyrannous and strong;
He struck with his o'ertaking wings,
And chased us south along.

With sloping masts and dipping prow,
As who pursued with yell and blow
Still treads the shadow of his foe,
And forward bends his head,
The ship drove fast, loud roared the blast,
And southward aye we fled.

And now there came both mist and snow,
And it grew wondrous cold:
And ice, mast-high, came floating by,
As green as emerald.

And through the drifts the snowy clifts
Did send a dismal sheen:
Nor shapes of men nor beasts we ken—
The ice was all between.

The ice was here, the ice was there,
The ice was all around:
It cracked and growled, and roared and howled,
Like noises in a swound!

At length did cross an Albatross,
Thorough the fog it came;
As if it had been a Christian soul,
We hailed it in God's name.

It ate the food it ne'er had eat,
And round and round it flew.
The ice did split with a thunder-fit;
The helmsman steered us through!

And a good south wind sprung up behind;
The Albatross did follow,
And every day, for food or play,
Came to the mariners' hollo!

In mist or cloud, on mast or shroud,
It perched for vespers nine;
Whiles all the night, through fog-smoke white,
Glimmered the white Moon-shine."

"God save thee, ancient Mariner!
From the fiends, that plague thee thus!—
Why look'st thou so?"—With my crossbow
I shot the ALBATROSS.

Part II

The Sun now rose upon the right:
Out of the sea came he,
Still hid in mist, and on the left
Went down into the sea.

And the good south wind still blew behind,
But no sweet bird did follow,
Nor any day for food or play
Came to the mariners' hollo!

And I had done a hellish thing,
And it would work 'em woe:
For all averred, I had killed the bird
That made the breeze to blow.
Ah wretch! said they, the bird to slay,
That made the breeze to blow!

Nor dim nor red, like God's own head,
The glorious Sun uprist:
Then all averred, I had killed the bird
That brought the fog and mist.
'Twas right, said they, such birds to slay,
That bring the fog and mist.

The fair breeze blew, the white foam flew,
The furrow followed free;
We were the first that ever burst
Into that silent sea.

Down dropped the breeze, the sails dropped
down,
'Twas sad as sad could be;
And we did speak only to break
The silence of the sea!

309

All in a hot and copper sky,
The bloody Sun, at noon,
Right up above the mast did stand,
No bigger than the Moon.

Day after day, day after day,
We stuck, nor breath nor motion;
As idle as a painted ship
Upon a painted ocean.

And the
Albatross begins
to be avenged.

Water, water, everywhere,
And all the boards did shrink;
Water, water, everywhere,
Nor any drop to drink.

The very deep did rot: O Christ!
That ever this should be!
Yea, slimy things did crawl with legs
Upon the slimy sea.

About, about, in reel and rout
The death-fires danced at night;
The water, like a witch's oils,
Burnt green, and blue and white.

A Spirit had
followed them;
one of the
invisible
inhabitants of this
planet,
neither departed souls nor angels; concerning whom the learned Jew, Josephus, and the Platonic
Constantinopolitan, Michael Psellus, may be consulted. They are very numerous, and there is no
climate or element without one or more.

And some in dreams assuréd were
Of the Spirit that plagued us so;
Nine fathom deep he had followed us
From the land of mist and snow.

And every tongue, through utter drought,
Was withered at the root;
We could not speak, no more than if
We had been choked with soot.

The shipmates, in their sore distress, would fain throw the whole guilt on the ancient Mariner:
Ah! well-a-day! what evil looks
Had I from old and young!
Instead of the cross, the Albatross
About my neck was hung.

in sign whereof they hang the dead sea bird round his neck.

Part III

There passed a weary time. Each throat
Was parched, and glazed each eye.
A weary time! a weary time!
How glazed each weary eye,
The ancient Mariner beholdeth a sign in the element afar off.
When looking westward, I beheld
A something in the sky.

At first it seemed a little speck,
And then it seemed a mist;
It moved and moved, and took at last
A certain shape, I wist.

A speck, a mist, a shape, I wist!
And still it neared and neared:
As if it dodged a water sprite,
It plunged and tacked and veered.

At its nearer approach, it seemeth him to be a ship; and at a dear ransom he freeth his speech from the bonds of thirst.
With throats unslaked, with black lips baked,
We could nor laugh nor wail;
Through utter drought all dumb we stood!
I bit my arm, I sucked the blood,
And cried, A sail! a sail!

A flash of joy;
With throats unslaked, with black lips baked,
Agape they heard me call:
Gramercy! they for joy did grin,
And all at once their breath drew in,
As they were drinking all.

See! see! (I cried) she tacks no more!
Hither to work us weal;
Without a breeze, without a tide,
She steadies with upright keel!

And horror
follows. For can
it be a ship that
comes onward
without wind or
tide?

The western wave was all aflame.
The day was well nigh done!
Almost upon the western wave
Rested the broad bright Sun;
When that strange shape drove suddenly
Betwixt us and the Sun.

It seemeth him
but the skeleton
of a ship.

And straight the Sun was flecked with bars,
(Heaven's Mother send us grace!)
As if through a dungeon gate he peered
With broad and burning face.

And its ribs are
seen as bars on
the face of the
setting Sun.

Alas! (thought I, and my heart beat loud)
How fast she nears and nears!
Are those *her* sails that glance in the Sun,
Like restless gossameres?

The
Specter-Woman
and her
Deathmate, and
no other on board
the skeleton ship.

Are those *her* ribs through which the Sun
Did peer, as through a grate?
And is that Woman all her crew?
Is that a DEATH? and are there two?
Is DEATH that woman's mate?

Like vessel, like
crew!

Her lips were red, *her* looks were free,
Her locks were yellow as gold:
Her skin was as white as leprosy,
The Nightmare LIFE-IN-DEATH was she,
Who thicks man's blood with cold.

Death and
Life-in-Death
have diced for the
ship's crew, and
she (the latter)
winneth the
ancient Mariner.

The naked hulk alongside came,
And the twain were casting dice;
"The game is done! I've won! I've won!"
Quoth she, and whistles thrice.

No twilight
within the courts
of the Sun.

The Sun's rim dips; the stars rush out:
At one stride comes the dark;
With far-heard whisper, o'er the sea,
Off shot the specter-bark.

At the rising of
the Moon,

We listened and looked sideways up!
Fear at my heart, as at a cup,
My lifeblood seems to sip!
The stars were dim, and thick the night,
The steersman's face by his lamp gleamed white;
From the sails the dew did drip—
Till clomb above the eastern bar
The hornéd Moon, with one bright star
Within the nether tip.

One after
another,

One after one, by the star-dogged Moon,
Too quick for groan or sigh,
Each turned his face with ghastly pang,
And cursed me with his eye.

His shipmates
drop down dead.

Four times fifty living men,
(And I heard nor sigh nor groan)
With heavy thump, a lifeless lump,
They dropped down one by one.

But Life-in-Death
begins her work
on the ancient
Mariner.

The souls did from their bodies fly—
They fled to bliss or woe!
And every soul, it passed me by,
Like the whizz of my cross-bow!

Part IV

The Wedding
Guest feareth
that a Spirit is
talking to him;

"I fear thee, ancient Mariner!
I fear thy skinny hand!
And thou art long, and lank, and brown,
As is the ribbed sea-sand.

313

I fear thee and thy glittering eye,
And thy skinny hand, so brown."—
Fear not, fear not, thou Wedding Guest!
This body dropped not down.

But the ancient
Mariner assureth
him of his bodily
life, and
proceedeth to
relate his horrible
penance.

Alone, alone, all, all alone,
Alone on a wide wide sea!
And never a saint took pity on
My soul in agony.

He despiseth the
creatures of the
calm,

The many men, so beautiful!
And they all dead did lie:
And a thousand thousand slimy things
Lived on; and so did I.

And envieth that
they should live,
and so many lie
dead.

I looked upon the rotting sea,
And drew my eyes away;
I looked upon the rotting deck,
And there the dead men lay.

I looked to heaven, and tried to pray;
But or ever a prayer had gushed,
A wicked whisper came, and made
My heart as dry as dust.

I closed my lids, and kept them close,
And the balls like pulses beat,
For the sky and the sea, and the sea and the sky
Lay like a load on my weary eye,
And the dead were at my feet.

But the curse
liveth for him in
the eye of the
dead men.

The cold sweat melted from their limbs,
Nor rot nor reek did they:
The look with which they looked on me
Had never passed away.

An orphan's curse would drag to hell
A spirit from on high;
But oh! more horrible than that
Is the curse in a dead man's eye!
Seven days, seven nights, I saw that curse,
And yet I could not die.

The moving Moon went up the sky,
And nowhere did abide:
Softly she was going up,
And a star or two beside—

Her beams bemocked the sultry main,
Like April hoar-frost spread;
But where the ship's huge shadow lay,
The charmèd water burnt alway
A still and awful red.

In his loneliness and fixedness he yearneth towards the journeying Moon, and the stars that still sojourn, yet still move onward; and everywhere the blue sky belongs to them, and is their appointed rest, and their native country and their own natural homes, which they enter unannounced, as lords that are certainly expected and yet there is a silent joy at their arrival.

By the light of the Moon he beholdeth God's creatures of the great calm.

Beyond the shadow of the ship,
I watched the water snakes:
They moved in tracks of shining white,
And when they reared, the elfish light
Fell off in hoary flakes.

Within the shadow of the ship
I watched their rich attire:
Blue, glossy green, and velvet black,
They coiled and swam; and every track
Was a flash of golden fire.

Their beauty and their happiness.

O happy living things! no tongue
Their beauty might declare:
A spring of love gushed from my heart,

He blesseth them in his heart.

And I blessed them unaware:
Sure my kind saint took pity on me,
And I blessed them unaware.

The spell begins
to break.

The self-same moment I could pray;
And from my neck so free
The Albatross fell off, and sank
Like lead into the sea.

Part V

Oh sleep! it is a gentle thing,
Beloved from pole to pole!
To Mary Queen the praise be given!
She sent the gentle sleep from Heaven,
That slid into my soul.

By grace of the
holy Mother, the
ancient Mariner
is refreshed with
rain.

The silly buckets on the deck,
That had so long remained,
I dreamt that they were filled with dew;
And when I awoke, it rained.

My lips were wet, my throat was cold,
My garments all were dank;
Sure I had drunken in my dreams,
And still my body drank.

I moved, and could not feel my limbs:
I was so light—almost
I thought that I had died in sleep,
And was a blesséd ghost.

He heareth
sounds and seeth
strange sights and
commotions in
the sky and the
element.

And soon I heard a roaring wind:
It did not come anear;
But with its sound it shook the sails,
That were so thin and sere.

The upper air burst into life!
And a hundred fire-flags sheen,
To and fro they were hurried about!
And to and fro, and in and out,
The wan stars danced between.

And the coming wind did roar more loud,
And the sails did sigh like sedge;
And the rain poured down from one black cloud;
The Moon was at its edge.

The thick black cloud was cleft, and still
The Moon was at its side:
Like waters shot from some high crag,
The lightning fell with never a jag,
A river steep and wide.

The loud wind never reached the ship,
Yet now the ship moved on!
Beneath the lightning and the Moon
The dead men gave a groan.

They groaned, they stirred, they all uprose,
Nor spake, nor moved their eyes;
It had been strange, even in a dream,
To have seen those dead men rise.

The helmsman steered, the ship moved on;
Yet never a breeze up-blew;
The mariners all 'gan work the ropes,
Where they were wont to do;
They raised their limbs like lifeless tools—
We were a ghastly crew.

The body of my brother's son
Stood by me, knee to knee:
The body and I pulled at one rope,
But he said nought to me.

"I fear thee, ancient Mariner!"
Be calm, thou Wedding Guest!
'Twas not those souls that fled in pain,
Which to their corses came again,
But a troop of spirits blest:

For when it dawned—they dropped their arms,
And clustered round the mast;
Sweet sounds rose slowly through their mouths,
And from their bodies passed.

Around, around, flew each sweet sound,
Then darted to the Sun;
Slowly the sounds came back again,
Now mixed, now one by one.

Sometimes a-dropping from the sky
I heard the sky-lark sing;
Sometimes all little birds that are,
How they seemed to fill the sea and air
With their sweet jargoning!

And now 'twas like all instruments,
Now like a lonely flute;
And now it is an angel's song,
That makes the heavens be mute.

It ceased; yet still the sails made on
A pleasant noise till noon,
A noise like of a hidden brook
In the leafy month of June,
That to the sleeping woods all night
Singeth a quiet tune.

Till noon we quietly sailed on,
Yet never a breeze did breathe:
Slowly and smoothly went the ship,
Moved onward from beneath.

The lonesome Spirit from the South Pole carries on the ship as far as the Line, in obedience to the angelic troop, but still requireth vengeance.

Under the keel nine fathom deep,
From the land of mist and snow,
The spirit slid: and it was he
That made the ship to go.
The sails at noon left off their tune,
And the ship stood still also.

The Sun, right up above the mast,
Had fixed her to the ocean:
But in a minute she 'gan stir,
With a short uneasy motion—
Backwards and forwards half her length
With a short uneasy motion.

Then like a pawing horse let go,
She made a sudden bound:
It flung the blood into my head,
And I fell down in a swound.

The Polar Spirit's fellow demons, the invisible inhabitants of the element, take part in his wrong; and two of them relate, one to the other, that penance long and heavy for the ancient Mariner hath been accorded to the Polar Spirit, who returneth southward.

How long in that same fit I lay,
I have not to declare;
But ere my living life returned,
I heard and in my soul discerned
Two voices in the air.

"Is it he?" quoth one, "Is this the man?
By him who died on cross,
With his cruel bow he laid full low
The harmless Albatross.

The spirit who bideth by himself
In the land of mist and snow,
He loved the bird that loved the man
Who shot him with his bow."

The other was a softer voice,
As soft as honey-dew:
Quoth he, "The man hath penance done,
And penance more will do."

Part VI

FIRST VOICE

FIRST VOICE

"But tell me, tell me! speak again,
Thy soft response renewing—
What makes that ship drive on so fast?
What is the ocean doing?"

SECOND VOICE

"Still as a slave before his lord,
The ocean hath no blast;
His great bright eye most silently
Up to the Moon is cast—

If he may know which way to go;
For she guides him smooth or grim.
See, brother, see! how graciously
She looketh down on him."

FIRST VOICE

The Mariner
hath been cast
into a trance; for
the angelic power
causeth the vessel
to drive
northward faster
than human life
could endure.

"But why drives on that ship so fast,
Without or wave or wind?"

SECOND VOICE

"The air is cut away before,
And closes from behind.

Fly, brother, fly! more high, more high!
Or we shall be belated:
For slow and slow that ship will go,
When the Mariner's trance is abated."

The supernatural
motion is
retarded; the
Mariner awakes,
and his penance
begins anew.

I woke, and we were sailing on
As in a gentle weather:
'Twas night, calm night, the moon was high;
The dead men stood together.

All stood together on the deck,
For a charnel-dungeon fitter:
All fixed on me their stony eyes,
That in the Moon did glitter.

The pang, the curse, with which they died,
Had never passed away:
I could not draw my eyes from theirs,
Nor turn them up to pray.

The curse is finally expiated.

And now this spell was snapped: once more
I viewed the ocean green,
And looked far forth, yet little saw
Of what had else been seen—

Like one, that on a lonesome road
Doth walk in fear and dread,
And having once turned round walks on,
And turns no more his head;
Because he knows, a frightful fiend
Doth close behind him tread.

But soon there breathed a wind on me,
Nor sound nor motion made:
Its path was not upon the sea,
In ripple or in shade.

It raised my hair, it fanned my cheek
Like a meadow-gale of spring—
It mingled strangely with my fears,
Yet it felt like a welcoming.

Swiftly, swiftly flew the ship,
Yet she sailed softly too:
Sweetly, sweetly blew the breeze—
On me alone it blew.

And the ancient Mariner beholdeth his native country.

Oh! dream of joy! is this indeed
The lighthouse top I see?
Is this the hill? is this the kirk?
Is this mine own countree?

We drifted o'er the harbor-bar,
And I with sobs did pray—
O let me be awake, my God!
Or let me sleep alway.

The harbor-bay was clear as glass,
So smoothly it was strewn!
And on the bay the moonlight lay,
And the shadow of the Moon.

The rock shone bright, the kirk no less,
That stands above the rock:
The moonlight steeped in silentness
The steady weathercock.

And the bay was white with silent light,
Till rising from the same,
Full many shapes, that shadows were,
In crimson colors came.

The angelic spirits leave the dead bodies,

A little distance from the prow
Those crimson shadows were:
I turned my eyes upon the deck—
Oh, Christ! what saw I there!

And appear in their own forms of light.

Each corse lay flat, lifeless and flat,
And, by the holy rood!
A man all light, a seraph-man,
On every corse there stood.

This seraph-band, each waved his hand:
It was a heavenly sight!
They stood as signals to the land,
Each one a lovely light;

This seraph-band, each waved his hand,
No voice did they impart—
No voice; but oh! the silence sank
Like music on my heart.

But soon I heard the dash of oars,
I heard the Pilot's cheer;
My head was turned perforce away
And I saw a boat appear.

The Pilot and the Pilot's boy,
I heard them coming fast:
Dear Lord in Heaven! it was a joy
The dead men could not blast.

I saw a third—I heard his voice:
It is the Hermit good!
He singeth loud his godly hymns
That he makes in the wood.
He'll shrieve my soul, he'll wash away
The Albatross's blood.

Part VII

The Hermit of
the Wood

This Hermit good lives in that wood
Which slopes down to the sea.
How loudly his sweet voice he rears!
He loves to talk with marineres
That come from a far countree.

He kneels at morn, and noon, and eve—
He hath a cushion plump:
It is the moss that wholly hides
The rotted old oak stump.

The skiff-boat neared: I heard them talk,
"Why, this is strange, I trow!
Where are those lights so many and fair,
That signal made but now?"

Approacheth the
ship with wonder.

"Strange, by my faith!" the Hermit said—
"And they answered not our cheer!
The planks looked warped! and see those sails,
How thin they are and sere!
I never saw aught like to them,
Unless perchance it were

323

Brown skeletons of leaves that lag
My forest-brook along;
When the ivy tod is heavy with snow,
And the owlet whoops to the wolf below,
That eats the she-wolf's young."

"Dear Lord! it hath a fiendish look,"
The Pilot made reply,
"I am a-feared"—"Push on, push on!"
Said the Hermit cheerily.

The boat came closer to the ship,
But I nor spake nor stirred;
The boat came close beneath the ship,
And straight a sound was heard.

The ship suddenly sinketh.

Under the water it rumbled on,
Still louder and more dread:
It reached the ship, it split the bay;
The ship went down like lead.

The ancient Mariner is saved in the Pilot's boat.

Stunned by that loud and dreadful sound,
Which sky and ocean smote,
Like one that hath been seven days drowned
My body lay afloat;
But swift as dreams, myself I found
Within the Pilot's boat.

Upon the whirl, where sank the ship,
The boat spun round and round;
And all was still, save that the hill
Was telling of the sound.

I moved my lips—the Pilot shrieked
And fell down in a fit;
The holy Hermit raised his eyes,
And prayed where he did sit.

324

I took the oars: the Pilot's boy,
Who now doth crazy go,
Laughed loud and long, and all the while
His eyes went to and fro.
"Ha! ha!" quoth he, "full plain I see,
The Devil knows how to row."

And now, all in my own countree,
I stood on the firm land!
The Hermit stepped forth from the boat,
And scarcely he could stand.

"O shrieve me, shrieve me, holy man!"
The Hermit crossed his brow.
"Say quick," quoth he, "I bid thee say—
What manner of man art thou?"

Forthwith this frame of mine was wrenched
With a woeful agony,
Which forced me to begin my tale;
And then it left me free.

Since then, at an uncertain hour,
That agony returns:
And till my ghastly tale is told,
This heart within me burns.

I pass, like night, from land to land;
I have strange power of speech;
That moment that his face I see,
I know the man that must hear me:
To him my tale I teach.

What loud uproar bursts from that door!
The wedding guests are there:
But in the garden-bower the bride
And bridemaids singing are:
And hark the little vesper bell,
Which biddeth me to prayer!

O Wedding Guest! this soul hath been
Alone on a wide wide sea:
So lonely 'twas, that God himself
Scarce seeméd there to be.

O sweeter than the marriage feast,
'Tis sweeter far to me,
To walk together to the kirk
With a goodly company!

To walk together to the kirk,
And all together pray,
While each to his great Father bends,
Old men, and babes, and loving friends
And youths and maidens gay!

Farewell, farewell! but this I tell
To thee, thou Wedding Guest!
He prayeth well, who loveth well
Both man and bird and beast.

He prayeth best, who loveth best
All things both great and small;
For the dear God who loveth us,
He made and loveth all.

The Mariner, whose eye is bright,
Whose beard with age is hoar,
Is gone: and now the Wedding Guest
Turned from the bridegroom's door.

He went like one that hath been stunned,
And is of sense forlorn:
A sadder and a wiser man,
He rose the morrow morn.

SAMUEL TAYLOR COLERIDGE

EXPLANATORY NOTES

Since some poems are more interesting when the reader knows how old they are, the dates of birth and death of all the poets represented in this book are printed after their names in the Index. In the following notes, the approximate dates of composition are given for poems over two hundred years old, and for a few others, simply to alert note-readers to a poem's origin in a culture long ago and far away.

2. *Sea Shell.* **Spanish Main:** the Caribbean Sea (once controlled by Spain), on the islands of which pirates hid chests of captured gold.

4. *Kidnap Poem.* **Jones Beach** and **Coney Island:** a public bathing beach on Long Island and a popular amusement center in Brooklyn, both in metropolitan New York.

6. *Down by the Salley Gardens.* **salley gardens:** a park in which willows grow, usually bordering a stream. **weirs:** dams made of earth.

7. *Cockles and Mussels.* **wheel-barrow:** pushcart. **cockles:** snails.

13. *The Country Mouse and the City Mouse.* **nicely regaling:** daintily feasting.

15. *The Giraffes.* **intercourse:** conversation, communication.

17. *When We Two Parted.* **light:** wanton, loose.

18. *I Wandered Lonely as a Cloud.* **jocund:** merry.

20. *Good Morrow.* Written about 1610. **pack . . . away:** leave at once. **prune:** preen, i.e., trim or make neat (your feathers). **stare:** starling.

22. *The Passionate Shepherd to His Love.* Written about 1558. **prove:** try, test, taste. **kirtle:** outer petticoat. **swains:** young men who work for the shepherds.

23. *The Nymph's Reply to the Shepherd.* Written about 1590. **nymph:** maiden. **Philomel:** the nightingale. **still:** always. **date:** end. **need:** lack.

25. *Those Winter Sundays.* **offices:** tasks, or rites, or ceremonies.

27. *Reason.* Josephine Miles, the poet, was so severely crippled that she could not walk alone.

28. *May.* **corn:** such grain as wheat.

32. *In Praise of a Contented Mind.* Written about 1580. This is a modernized version. **that world affords or grows by kind:** that is

offered by either human society or the world of nature. **though much I want**: though I lack much. **no wily wit to salve a sore**: no sharp wit with which to hurt an enemy and thereby ease my hurt. **for why**: because. **my stay**: my support. **look what**: whatever. **I leave**: I leave behind me when I die. **pine**: waste away.

34. *Paul Revere's Ride.* This poem concerns the beginning of the War of Independence in 1775, when the British Royal Governor of the Massachusetts Bay Colony and Commander of the King's troops in North America decided to send a detachment of about 800 men from Boston to Concord, 15 miles away, to destroy the military supplies that the colonists had stored there and, en route, to seize John Hancock and Samuel Adams, leaders of the colonial rebels, in the village of Lexington. Word of the governor's plan got out, and as the poem tells us, a Boston silversmith named Paul Revere managed to alert all the colonists along the route of the British. Revere and the British soldiers were both in Boston at the time. Revere rowed across the Charles River to Charlestown, where he waited for the signal that would tell him whether the British detachment was going to proceed west from Boston "by land" or from a point north of Boston which they would reach by crossing the Charles River in boats ("by sea"). Revere got a good start on the British troops and was able to alert all the villages and farms from Medford to Lexington to Concord, all in the county of Middlesex. As a result, the colonists' resistance was severe enough to force the commander of the British detachment to send for reinforcements. And when the British light infantry arrived in Lexington early in the morning, it found itself confronted on the village green by 60 or 70 armed "Minute Men," drawn up in line of battle. When the British commander ordered the Minute Men to disperse and they refused, someone fired a shot that was the first shot in a war that lasted six years and brought about the independence of the American colonies (see Ralph Waldo Emerson's "Concord Hymn," p. 129)

39. *The Owl and the Pussy-Cat.* **five-pound note**: a piece of English paper money, larger than an American five-dollar bill. **mince**: hash. **runcible spoon**: a three-pronged fork, with a cutting edge, shaped like a spoon.

48. *Barbara Frietchie.* This poem, published shortly before the end of the American Civil War, was based on what is now considered an apocryphal story. What is factual is that after defeating Union forces

at the Second Battle of Bull Run, on August 30, 1862, Confederate forces under General "Stonewall" Jackson pursued the Union forces north through the town of Fredericksburg, Virginia. Whittier's poem, popular for over a century, praises both a Union heroine, "Barbara Frietchie," and a Confederate hero, the brilliant strategist, General Jackson.

51. *The World Is Too Much With Us.* **world:** the man-made world of affairs, the daily life of human society. **is too much with us:** preoccupies us, concerns us, too much. **sordid boon:** degrading gift. **Pagan:** non-Christian. **suckled in a creed outworn:** brought up in a religion no longer practiced. **Proteus** and **Triton:** Greek gods who lived in the sea.

52. *O Taste and See.* **O taste and see:** "O taste and see that the Lord is good." (Psalms 34:8).

53. *O Mistress Mine.* From *Twelfth Night* (Act II, scene iii). **mistress:** beloved. **sweeting:** little sweet one. **plenty:** the line means that waiting will not increase your value.

54. *The Pied Piper of Hamelin.* Written to amuse the son of one of the poet's friends, who was "confined to the house by illness," and to "give him a subject for illustrative drawings." **pied:** describes the piper's "queer coat" and scarf, "half of yellow and half of red." A pied coat is made of two or more colors, checkered or arranged in patches, as in a clown's costume.

STANZA IV. **a plate of turtle:** a bowl of turtle soup.

STANZA V. **his kith and kin:** his native country or his family, that is, where he came from. **the Trump of Doom's tone:** the trumpets announcing the end of the world and The Last Judgment.

STANZA VII. **his commentary:** in his *Commentaries* Caesar recorded his conquest of Gaul (the ancient name for a region within what is now called Western Europe, then a barbarian territory). **train-oil:** whale or fish oil. **psaltery:** a stringed instrument mentioned in the Bible and still played as recently as a few centuries ago. **drysaltery:** a store where, among other things, meats and groceries were sold. **nuncheon:** snack. **puncheon:** a large cask. **staved:** broken open.

STANZA X. **bate a stiver:** come down a nickel, or a penny.

STANZA XI. **ribald:** rogue, rascal.

STANZA XII. **at pitching and hustling:** around the pitchmen and hustlers at a fair.

STANZA XIII. **the High Street:** main street.

STANZA XIV. **A text which says that heaven's gate/Opes to the rich
. . . :** The lines in the Bible (Matthew 19:24) read as follows: "It
is easier for a camel to go through the eye of a needle, than for a rich
man to enter into the kingdom of God."

64. *Against Idleness and Mischief.* First published in 1715 in Isaac
Watts's *Divine Songs for Children*, the first book of English poems
written especially for children. In *Alice in Wonderland*, when Alice
tries to remember this poem, it comes out wrong, as follows:

> How doth the little crocodile
> Improve his shining tail,
> And pour the waters of the Nile
> On every golden scale!
>
> How cheerfully he seems to grin,
> How neatly spreads his claws,
> And welcomes little fishes in,
> With gently smiling jaws!

65. *Emily Jane.* **potato poll:** head made of a potato.

66. *Annabel Lee.* Probably written shortly before the poet's death.

68. *since feeling is first.* **syntax:** proper order or correct form.

69. *In These Dissenting Times.* **stand of greens:** a standing growth of
(in this context) collards, or mustard or turnip leaves.

78. *Snake.* **And I thought of the albatross:** The thought of killing the
snake reminds the speaker of a story about an old seafarer who killed
an albatross and thereby brought a terrifying curse upon himself, his
crew, and his ship. The story is told in a well-known poem by Samuel
Taylor Coleridge, "The Rime of the Ancient Mariner" (see p. 306).

83. *The Walrus and the Carpenter.* From *Through the Looking-Glass.*

87. *God moves in a mysterious way.* Written about 1770, and first published in Cowper's *Olney Hymns* (1779).

88. *Hymn to Cynthia.* Written about 1600, to be sung by Hesperus, the
Evening Star, in a masque (a short, dramatic musical entertainment)
entitled *Cynthia's Revels*, written to be presented on the estate of
a noble family. The first stanza of his song is addressed to Cynthia,
goddess of the moon and of chastity, who is to hold court in the sky.
In the second stanza Hesperus addresses the earth, asking her not to
come between the sun and the moon, and thus cause an eclipse. In
the third, Hesperus addresses Cynthia in her role as huntress—and

as protector of the creatures of the forest, especially the hart or deer. Written during the reign of Queen Elizabeth I, "the virgin Queen," this lyric would be understood as praise of her. A reader with a good ear for melody need know none of these facts to enjoy the verbal magic of this masterpiece.

91. *Ducks' Ditty.* From *The Wind in the Willows.*

93. *My Heart Leaps Up.* **natural piety**: a nonreligious reverence for, or devotion to, or awe of nature, and its manifestations, such as rainbows.

95. *The Deacon's Masterpiece.* Oliver Wendell Holmes was a professor in the Harvard Medical School, one of the founders of the *Atlantic Monthly*, an essayist, a poet, and the father of Supreme Court Justice Oliver Wendell Holmes. This poem, written in 1879, will still seem humorous to readers who take their cue from its subtitle "A Logical Story." Holmes satirizes people who take pride in their superior powers of reason but fail to see that their reasoning is based on a faulty assumption. **shay**: chaise; a two-wheel, horse-drawn buggy. *Georgius Secundus:* George II, King of England (1727– 1760). **Lisbon-town**: capital city of Portugal, devastated by an earthquake in 1755. **Braddock's army**: British forces commanded by General Edward Braddock, defeated in the French and Indian War in a battle near what is now Pittsburgh, Pennsylvania. **felloe**: the part of a wheel into which the outer ends of the spokes fit. **thills**: the shafts between which the horse is harnessed. **linchpin**: a steel pin that goes through the end of the axle to keep the wheel on. **runs at large**: doesn't belong to any particular person. **whipple-tree**: whiffletree, a bar to which are fastened the traces (or strong leather straps) by means of which the horse pulls the buggy. *encore:* as well.

101. *The Sluggard.* Like "Against Idleness and Mischief" (see p. 64), this poem was published in 1716 in Isaac Watts' *Divine Songs for Children.* When Alice, in *Alice in Wonderland*, was asked by the Mock Turtle to "repeat," that is, to recite, " 'Tis the voice of the sluggard," the "words came very queer indeed":

> 'Tis the voice of the Lobster: I heard him declare
> "You have baked me too brown, I must sugar my hair."
> As a duck with his eyelids, so he with his nose
> Trims his belt and his buttons, and turns out his toes.
> When the sands are all dry, he is gay as a lark,

And will talk in contemptuous tones of the Shark:
But when the tide rises and sharks are around,
His voice has a timid and tremulous sound.

102. *We Are Seven.* **cottage girl**: one who lives in a humble dwelling, the house of a laborer.

105. *To the Virgins, to Make Much of Time.* Written about 1630. **virgins**: young unmarried women.

109. *Western Wind.* Written about 1300, one of the oldest lyrics in the English language.

110. *Egrets.* **paperbarks**: birch trees.

111. *The Harlot's House.* **Treues Liebes Herz:** "Heart of True Love," the name of a Viennese waltz by Johann Strauss. **arabesque**: a pose in classical ballet in which the dancer balances on one leg by extending one arm forward and the other arm and leg behind. **sidling through the slow quadrille**: moving sideways, obliquely, in one of the figures of a formal, or ballroom-style, square dance. **saraband**: a polite version of what was originally a lively, vigorous dance.

115. *Cavalry Crossing a Ford.* **guidon flags**: small flags or banners for signaling or identifying military units. During the Civil War Walt Whitman visited his wounded brother in a camp near the site of the Battle of Fredericksburg.

116. *Contingency.* **contingency**: what the events in the poem exemplify. The definitions in the *American Heritage Dictionary* are: "An event that may occur but that is not likely or intended. The condition of being dependent upon chance; uncertainty; fortuitousness."

117. *Dust of Snow.* **rued**: wished had never been.

119. *Boy at the Window.* **bitumen eyes**: eyes made of pieces of coal.

122. *When I was one-and-twenty.* **in vain**: without any effect or consequences. **rue**: regret.

124. *Soliloquy of a Tortoise. . . .* **soliloquy**: a speech delivered aloud in solitude.

125. *To Daffodils.* Written about 1630. **but to the Evensong**: only until time for the evening church service known as evensong or vespers.

126. *The Outlandish Knight.* **outlandish**: foreign, barbarous. **fee**: possessions. **stays**: corset. **Holland smock**: linen undergarment, a slip.

128. *The 1st.* **the 1st**: the first of the month, moving day for renters, especially poor, urban people—in this case, blacks.

129. *Concord Hymn.* **Concord**: the village in Massachusetts where the American Revolutionary War began. See the notes to Henry Wadsworth Longfellow's "Paul Revere's Ride" on p. 34.

130. *Believe Me, If All Those Endearing Young Charms.* **sunflower**: a heliotropic plant—that is, one whose flower turns during the day in order to face the sun.

134. *The Foggy Dew.* **foggy** (perhaps): dank, moist in an unhealthful way.

136. *Answer to a Child's Question.* During mating season the male skylark, unlike most other birds, sings on the wing.

138. *The Owl.* **sail**: the vanes or arms on the wheel of a windmill. **rarely**: extraordinarily fine. **roundelay**: a song in which a line or phrase is continually repeated.

139. *The Water-Ousel.* **water-ousel**: a plump, thick-plumaged bird related to the thrush. When it perches, it sometimes makes a jerky motion, as in "her quick, imitative curtsies." It walks into and under the water in search of insects, and from this bobbing action it is called a dipper. **weir**: dam.

140. *Recuerdo.* The title means a recollection, or memory.

144. *The Pear Tree.* **waste-man**: unskilled factory laborer, who collects and removes waste products.

146. *Danny Deever.* Written about 1890. **Files-on-Parade**: a private in the British army.

148. *The Lake Isle of Innisfree.* **wattles**: interwoven branches that reinforce the clay.

149. *The River-Merchant's Wife: A Letter.* This is a free translation by Ezra Pound of a seventh-century Chinese poem. Pound attributed the original to Rihaku.

151. *Thirteen Ways of Looking at a Blackbird.* **Haddam**: a town in Connecticut, home state of the poet. **bawds of euphony**: pimps or procuresses of pleasing sounds.

154. *O What Is That Sound.* **wheeling**: turning.

156. *Water Ouzel.* **The ridiculous ouzel**: see note to Mary Webb's "The Water-Ousel" on p. 139 above.

162. *My Last Duchess.* The factual grounds of this imagined account are as follows: In the middle of the sixteenth century the Duke of Ferrara married a fourteen-year-old girl of noble birth (the "last duchess," whose portrait hangs on the wall). She died under suspicious circumstances three years later, and shortly thereafter he mar-

ried the daughter of the Count of Tyrol. In this poem, the fictional-ized Duke addresses the Count of Tyrol's emissary. **last:** most recent. **favor:** gift bestowed as a token of love, such as a brooch, necklace, or pendant.

169. *The Fish.* **isinglass:** thin, transparent sheets of mica (a mineral) that looks a little like the material of fish scales. Before the age of transparent plastic film it was used for such things as windows in tents. The poet may remember that it grew yellow with age and that it scratched easily.

174. *Macavity: the Mystery Cat.* **levitation:** making things float in air. **fakir:** an itinerant Hindu magician, among whose tricks is levitation.

178. *The Lady of Shalott.*

PART I. **wold:** open land. **Camelot:** the site of the palace of the legendary King Arthur of ancient Britain. **blow:** bloom. **dusk and shiver/ Through the wave:** darken and make ripples on the water. **imbow-ers:** surrounds with foliage, as in a bower. **margin:** bank of the river. **trailed:** towed. **shallop:** small, light boat.

PART II. **stay:** should stop. **mirror:** The Lady stands with her back to the window, by the light of which she sees to work at the loom standing vertically in front of her. To see the progress of the pattern she is weaving, she must look in the mirror on the other side of the loom, because what she sees immediately in front of her is the back side of the tapestry. The mirror reflects the life outside her room as well as the work of art she is weaving. **churls:** lower-class people. **market girls:** women who sell in the market. **pad:** utility riding horse.

PART III. **brazen greaves:** brass leg armor. **a red-cross knight forever kneeled / To a lady in his shield:** Lancelot's coat of arms, dis-played on his shield. The first red-cross knight was St. George, the patron saint of England; after killing a dragon, he married his lady, who was the personification of holiness. **gemmy:** adorned with gems. **blazoned baldric:** a sash covered with heraldic insignia, worn diagonally across the chest.

185. *A True Account of Talking to the Sun at Fire Island.* **Fire Island:** a long sandspit off the southern shore of Long Island, near New York City; a summer resort popular among artists and writers. **Mayakovsky:** a famous Russian poet (1893–1930).

192. *Afton Water.* **braes:** hillsides. **stock-dove:** wild pigeon. **lapwing:** plover, whose "song" is a shrill cry. **cot:** cottage. **lea:** meadow. **birk:** birch. **lave:** wash. **lays:** songs.

193. *Song.* **haply**: perhaps.

196. *Journey of the Magi.* T. S. Eliot enclosed the first five lines of this poem in quotation marks because they are almost word for word from a Christmas sermon written by a great seventeenth-century prose writer and bishop, Lancelot Andrewes, one of the translators who produced the King James, or Authorized, English Bible. **Magi**: the "wise men" or priests who came to Bethlehem from "the east" to worship Jesus, the newborn King of Israel. **galled**: made sore by the chafing of the saddles. **dispensation**: religious system or code of moral law.

198. *Winter.* **keel**: stir. **saw**: proverb, or wise saying. **crabs**: crab apples, roasting by the fire.

199. *Song from "Pippa Passes."* A snail is a handsome little creature and, seen on the leaf of a hawthorn bush in bloom, it presents to the poet another reason to believe that all's right with the world.

200. *The Old Man's Comforts and How He Gained Them.* Written about 1800. This poem would not have found a place in this collection had it not been the poem the Caterpillar commanded Alice, in Wonderland, to repeat and that Alice was trying to repeat when she produced instead "You Are Old, Father William" (see next poem), a nonsense poem from Alice's point of view, but a parody from the point of view of Lewis Carroll. Southey's poem may sound to us, as it sounded to Carroll, too didactic to be very poetic, but just as Alice's version is more interesting if we know Southey's poem, so Southey's poem is more interesting if we know its source, or what was in Southey's mind when he wrote it—a famous (and beautiful) passage in the Bible—Chapter 12 of the book of Ecclesiastes; or The Preacher: "Remember now thy Creator in the days of thy youth, while the evil days come not, nor the years draw nigh, when thou shalt say I have no pleasure in them; While the sun, or the light, or the moon or the stars, be not darkened, nor the clouds return not after the rain: In the day the keepers of the house [your arms and legs] shall tremble, and the strong men shall bow themselves, and the grinders [teeth] cease because they are few, and those that look out of the windows [eyes] be darkened, And the doors [lips] shall be shut in the streets, when the sound of the grinding is low, and he shall rise up at the voice of the bird [because in his old age he's a light sleeper], and all the daughters of music shall be brought low; Also when they shall be afraid of that which is high [hills are too

steep because of their feebleness], and fears shall be in the way, and the almond tree shall flourish [their hair will be white like the almond tree in blossom], and the grasshopper shall be a burden, and desire shall fail: because man goeth to his long home, and the mourners go about the streets: Or ever the silver cord be loosed, and the golden bowl [holding the oil that fuels the lamp] be broken, or the pitcher be broken at the fountain, or the wheel be broken at the cistern [these may all be metaphors for death]. Then shall the dust return to the earth as it was: and the spirit shall return unto God who gave it."

203. *Jabberwocky.* A poem discovered by Alice near the beginning of *Through the Looking-Glass* (1872).

205. *The King of Yvetot.* An adaptation of a French song by Pierre-Jean de Béranger (1780–1857), a *chansonnier*, a composer and singer of popular songs, some of them political satire. Thackeray's translation was published about 1850. *Yvetot* is pronounced "eve-a-toe." **Pater Patriae:** father of his country.

211. *Bonny George Campbell.* This is a Scottish ballad, a song handed down orally for generations from as far back, perhaps, as the sixteenth century, when the noble Campbell was murdered for political reasons. **greeting fu' sair:** weeping very sorrowfully. **riving:** tearing. **toom:** empty.

212. *To the Thawing Wind.* **Southwester:** spring winds from the west, in England and America, bring everything to life and fertility. See the anonymous poem "Western Wind," on p. 109.

215. *A Birthday.* **in a watered shoot:** on the edge of a rapid. **halcyon:** perfectly calm. **dais:** platform, at the end of a room, on which stands a throne, or a seat for an honored guest. **vair:** gray-and-white squirrel fur used for trimming ceremonial gowns. **fleurs-de-lys:** three-petaled lilies, often used in ornamental design as a heraldic emblem; the fleur-de-lys is found in coats-of-arms and was the sign of the royal family of France.

216. *The Brook.* **coot and hern:** aquatic birds such as the moorhen and heron. **bicker:** hurry, or sparkle or flicker. **thorps:** villages. **shingly bars:** sandbars covered with pebbles.

219. *To an Athlete Dying Young.* **threshold** and **lintel:** in life his friends carried him home and set him down at the doorsill of his house; now they bring him to the grave, the doorway to the house of the dead, inhabited by "shades," or ghosts, hence **the shady night** and **the sill** (threshold) **of shade.** The top member (lintel) of the

frame of the "door" to his new home (i.e., the grave) is lower than that of his house in life. **fields**: playing fields (now the spirit of the dead athlete has gone to what in Greek myth was called the Elysian fields). **rout**: band, company. **still-defended**: forever-defended. **challenge-cup**: a trophy that you hold as long as you can defeat those who challenge you.

223. *Poppies in October.* Poppies do not flower in the wild as late as October. The poet sees them in a flower vendor's cart on the sidewalk of a London street on a cloudy autumn morning. **Palely and flamily/Igniting its carbon monoxides**: The lower levels of the atmosphere do contain carbon monoxide, and this compound may be oxidized way up there in the sky, though not literally in flames. **bowlers**: bowler hats, worn by men who work in the financial district in London.

224. *The Wraggle Taggle Gypsies.* **bravely**: beautifully.

228. *"The Ousel Cock"—.* **ousel cock**: male blackbird—not related to the water-ousel. The title is quoted from a song in Shakespeare's *A Midsummer Night's Dream* (Act III, scene ii):

> The woosel-cock, so black of hue,
> With orange-tawny bill . . .

229. *Snow in the Suburbs.* **palings**: the vertical sticks that make a fence. **inurns**: buries.

231. *The Gallows.* **a thief and a murderer**: crows carry off all kinds of things that catch their attention, and they eat the eggs and the young of other birds. **could both talk and do**: the magpie, a large, aggressive, loud bird belonging to the family of crows, is not only a thief and a murderer, it also chatters endlessly.

236. *Little Trotty Wagtail.* **trotty**: busy, lively, bustling. **pudge**: puddle.

242. *Jephson Gardens.* **Jephson Gardens**: a park in the town where the poet was born and lived as a child.

245. *There Was a Knight.* **Cather banks**: perhaps Catley Burn, a stream near Roxburgh, in Scotland; or Cathkin Braes, hills near Glasgow; or Cathcart in Lanark; or Caterthun Hills in Farfar; or some other stream or hill popular as a beautiful, romantic spot. **bonnie broom**: a pretty flowering bush. **pies**: magpies, a noisy kind of crow, some of whom have green plumage. **Clootie**: Satan.

252. *The Cowboy's Lament.* **Laredo**: a city in Texas.

258. *There is no Frigate like a Book.* **Coursers:** swift horses. **offence:** annoyance. **frugal:** economical, inexpensive.

266. *On the Grasshopper and Cricket.* Keats wrote this sonnet in less than fifteen minutes one evening when he and a friend agreed to see who could most quickly compose a sonnet on the same subject. **he has never done:** he is never finished.

267. *Gracious Goodness.* **telling:** counting.

275. *The Solitary Reaper.* Written in 1805. Because the song sung by the young Scottish woman is in the Gaelic language, the poet does not know "what she sings." **lay:** song.

278. *The Splendor Falls.* **scar:** bare place on the side of a mountain.

279. *The Fairies.* **rushy glen:** a valley thick with plants that grow in marshes, such as cattails and wild flags. **Columbkill:** a glen in the western part of County Donegal, in Ireland.

281. *La Belle Dame sans Merci.* Written about 1820. The title means "The Beautiful Lady Without Mercy." **sedge:** grasslike plants that grow in wet places. **meads:** meadows. **zone:** belt. **manna dew:** a sweet juice obtained by incision of an ash tree. **grot:** grotto, cave. **latest:** last. **thrall:** slavery. **gloam:** twilight.

285. *Fear No More the Heat o' the Sun.* A song from Shakespeare's play *Cymbeline* (Act IV, scene ii). It is a dirge sung by two friends standing by the body of a friend whom they believe to be dead. One friend sings the first stanza, the second sings the second, and then they sing the remaining lines alternately, in a way that makes the performance seem ceremonial. **scepter, learning, physic:** monarchs, learned people, physicians. **thunder stone:** thunderbolt, the stone or shaft that was thought to make a flash as it was hurled through the atmosphere. **consign to thee:** submit to the same terms as you; do as you have done. **exorciser:** one who by magic spells removes evil spirits. **ghost unlaid:** the ghost of someone never correctly buried and hence free to roam the earth. **consummation:** fulfillment, completion.

286. *Under the Waterfall.* **purl:** the murmuring sound made by a shallow stream passing over stones. **three spans:** about 27 inches. **in stir of:** in times of international commotion. **throe:** pang of emotion.

288. *A Glass of Beer.* **The lanky hank of a she:** the skinny piece of rope of a woman. **gill:** quarter of a pint (a very small drink).

290. *But He Was Cool . . .* **tikis:** carved miniature human figures worn on necklaces. **swahili:** a language used in eastern and central Africa,

chiefly in Tanzania. **yoruba:** one of the languages used in West Africa, chiefly in Nigeria. **hip:** understand.

299. *Say Not the Struggle Nought Availeth.* Written about 1850. **flooding in:** moving of the tide. **main:** ocean.

300. *The Night Piece, to Julia.* Written about 1640. **glowworm:** firefly. **will-o'-the-wisp:** a phosphorescent light produced by gases generated in marshes. Because it flits about, according to folklore it mischievously misleads people who follow it. **slowworm:** lizard. **cumber:** impede.

301. *The Twa Brothers.* A Scottish ballad, one of many versions of this story, found in many languages. **twa:** two. **warsle:** wrestle. **gied:** gave. **burn:** brook. **aye:** always. **kirk-yard:** churchyard. **ta'en:** taken. **gin:** if. **lo'e:** love.

303. *The Fallow Deer at the Lonely House.* **fallow deer:** a common species of deer, smaller than the red deer, which takes its name from the color of its coat, which is fallow, yellow. **By the fender-brink:** up close to the fire in the fireplace. A fender is a low metal guard placed on a hearth to prevent hot coals from rolling onto the floor.

304. *The Song of Wandering Aengus.* **Aengus:** According to Yeats, "The man in my poem who has a hazel wand may have been Aengus, Master of Love," whom Yeats elsewhere identified as the "God of Youth, beauty and poetry." **a little silver trout:** explained by Yeats in the following note:

The Tribes of the goddess Danu can take all shapes, and those that are in the waters take often the shape of fish. A woman of Burren, in Galway, says, "There are more of them in the sea than on the land, and they sometimes try to come over the side of the boat in the form of fishes, for they can take their choice shape." At other times they are beautiful women; and another Galway woman says, "Surely those things are in the sea as well as on land. My father was out fishing one night off Tyrone. And something came beside the boat that had eyes shining like candles. And then a wave came in, and a storm rose all in a minute, and whatever was in the wave, the weight of it had like to sink the boat. And then they saw that it was a woman in the sea that had the shining eyes. So my father went to the priest, and he bid him always to take a drop of holy water and a pinch of salt out in the boat with him, and nothing could harm him."

The poem was suggested to me by a Greek folk song; but the folk belief of Greece is very like that of Ireland, and I certainly thought, when I wrote it, of Ireland, and of the spirits that are in

Ireland. An old man who was cutting a quickset hedge near Gort, in Galway, said, only the other day, "One time I was cutting timber over in Inchy, and about eight o'clock one morning, when I got there, I saw a girl picking nuts, with her hair hanging down over her shoulders; brown hair; and she had a good clean face, and she was tall, and nothing on her head, and her dress no way gaudy, but simple. And when she felt me coming she gathered herself up, and was gone, as if the earth had swallowed her up. And I followed her, and looked for her, but I never could see her again from that day to this, never again."

The county Galaway people use the word "clean" in its old sense of fresh and comely.

—Quoted by A. N. Jeffares in his *Commentary on the Collected Poems of W. B. Yeats*, from Yeats's *Wind among the Reeds*.

a glimmering girl: Maude Gonne, a woman with whom Yeats had fallen in love a few years before writing this poem. When he first met her, "her complexion was luminous," Yeats recalled, "like that of apple-blossoms through which the light falls." And he remembered her "standing that first day by a great heap of such blossoms," which she was arranging in a vase.

306. *The Rime of the Ancient Mariner*. Written about 1800. The title means "The Poem of the Old Sailor." The poet placed at the head of the poem a Latin epigraph, a translation of which follows:

I readily believe that there are more invisible than visible Natures in the universe. But who will explain for us the family of all these beings, and the ranks and relations and distinguishing features and functions of each? What do they do? What places do they inhabit? The human mind has always sought the knowledge of these things, but never attained it. Meanwhile I do not deny that it is helpful sometimes to contemplate in the mind, as on a tablet, the image of a greater and better world, lest the intellect, habituated to the petty things of daily life, narrow itself and sink wholly into trivial thoughts. But at the same time we must be watchful for the truth and keep a sense of proportion, so that we may distinguish the certain from the uncertain, day from night.

—Thomas Burnet, *Archaeologiae philosophicae* (1692)

argument: summary of the plot. This summary, as well as the explanatory notes in the margin of the page, is by Coleridge.

PART I. **Gallants**: cavaliers, gentlemen. **loon**: worthless or stupid fellow. **eftsoons**: at once. **kirk**: church. **Till over the mast at noon**: till the ship had reached the equator. **aye**: always. **swound**: swoon, fainting fit. **shroud**: rope that braces the mast. **vespers nine**: nine evening worship services.

PART II. **The sun now rose upon the right**: The ship had changed direction. Having previously sailed south, it was now rounding the tip of South America and heading north into the Pacific Ocean. **averred**: declared very positively. **death-fires**: St. Elmo's fire, light seen on a ship's spars and rigging, caused by atmospheric electricity.

PART III. **wist**: knew. **gramercy**: an expression of surprise, as in "mercy on us!" **work us weal**: bring us benefit. **gossameres**: cobwebs floating in the air. **specter-bark**: phantom ship. **The hornéd Moon, with one bright star**: a bad omen.

PART IV. **Nor rot nor reek did they**: they neither rotted nor stank. **main**: sea. **hoar-frost**: frozen dew, white frost.

PART V. **Mary Queen**: Mary the mother of Jesus. **silly buckets**: blessed (because they were about to receive rain from Heaven) or, perhaps, useless or empty. **sere**: worn. **a hundred fire-flags sheen**: the Southern Lights *(aurora australis)*, seen in the Southern Hemisphere, as the Northern Lights *(aurora borealis)* are seen in the Northern. **sedge**: a tall, coarse grasslike plant. **corses**: corpses. **jargoning**: warbling. **honey-dew**: a sweet substance found on the leaves of certain plants.

PART VI. **charnel-dungeon**: underground vault where the bodies of the dead are deposited. **steeped**: drenched. **rood**: cross. **seraph**: angel. **Pilot**: harbor pilot, who comes aboard to steer the ship into port. **shrieve**: shrive, grant absolution to.

PART VII. **lag**: move slowly. **ivy tod**: clump of ivy. **of sense forlorn**: deserted by his senses.

ACKNOWLEDGMENTS

Every effort has been made to trace the ownership of all copyrighted material and to secure the necessary permissions to reprint these selections. In the event of any question arising as to the use of any material, the editor and the publisher, while expressing deep regret for any inadvertent error, will be happy to make the necessary correction in future printings. Thanks are due to the following for permission to reprint the copyrighted materials listed below:

A. R. AMMONS: "Contingency" and "World" are reprinted from *Collected Poems, 1951–1971*, by A. R. Ammons, by permission of W. W. Norton & Company, Inc. Copyright © 1972 by A. R. Ammons. "Spruce Woods" is reprinted from *Worldly Hopes, Poems by A. R. Ammons*, by permission of W. W. Norton & Company, Inc. Copyright © 1982 by A. R. Ammons.

JOHN ASHBERY: "The Instruction Manual" from *Selected Poems* by John Ashbery. Copyright © 1985 by John Ashbery. All rights reserved. Reprinted by permission of Viking Penguin, Inc., and Carcanet Press Limited.

W. H. AUDEN: "O What Is That Sound." Copyright 1937 and renewed 1965 by W. H. Auden. Reprinted from *W. H. Auden: Collected Poems*, edited by Edward Mendelson, by permission of Random House, Inc., and Faber & Faber Ltd.

HILAIRE BELLOC: "The Frog" and "The Vulture" from *Cautionary Tales* by Hilaire Belloc. Published in 1941 by Alfred A. Knopf, Inc. Reprinted by permission of the publisher, and Gerald Duckworth & Co. Ltd.

ELIZABETH BISHOP: "The Fish" from *The Complete Poems 1927–1979* by Elizabeth Bishop. Copyright © 1979, 1983 by Alice Helen Methfessel. Reprinted by permission of Farrar, Straus and Giroux, Inc.

MORRIS BISHOP: "Sales Talk for Annie" from *A Book of Bishop* by Morris Bishop. Copyright 1954 by Morris Bishop. Reprinted by permission of Doubleday, a division of Bantam, Doubleday, Dell Publishing Group, Inc.

GWENDOLYN BROOKS: "A Song in the Front Yard," "Pete at the Zoo," and "We Real Cool" from *Blacks* by Gwendolyn Brooks. Copyright © 1987 by Gwendolyn Brooks. "Narcissa" from *Bronzeville Boys and Girls*, copyright © 1956 by Gwendolyn Brooks. All four poems reprinted by permission of Gwendolyn Brooks.

JOHN CLARE: "Little Trotty Wagtail" from *The Poems of John Clare*, published by J. M. Dent & Sons, Ltd. Reprinted by permission of the publisher.

343

344

INDEX

355